1988

INTEGRATING
THE
PRIMARY CURRICULUM

Social Studies and Children's Literature

by
Tom and Meredith McGowan

Special Literature Press
Indianapolis, Indiana

(Literature and Library Series)

HIEBERT LIBRARY 61612
Fresno Pacific College - M. B. Seminary
Fresno, Calif 93702

Copyright© 1988 by Tom and Meredith McGowan

All rights reserved. No part of this publication may be reproduced in any form without permission in writing from the publisher, except by a reviewer who may quote brief passages in a review.

Illustrations copyright© 1988 by Deborah Mitzlaff

DEDICATION

For Claire and Andy, whose arrival transformed us from couple to family and reminded us that children are America's greatest resource.

ACKNOWLEDGEMENTS

So many people supported our writing of this activity book in so many ways that it is impossible to give them all the credit they deserve in so limited a space. We can only thank a few who come immediately to mind:

The children's librarians at the Vigo County Public Library, Terre Haute, Indiana, for discovering some good books that we might otherwise have missed.

The staff at the Sullivan County Public Library, Sullivan, Indiana, for their suggestions and for mailing such polite overdue notices for the selections we kept too long.

The able teachers and excited young people we've observed in numerous elementary classrooms for inspiring us to create distinctive and meaningful activities.

Our publisher, Jack Champlin, for smiling through missed deadlines and encouraging a project that departs from "traditional" approaches to social studies teaching.

CONTENTS

WITHDRAWN

INTRODUCTION

THE CASE FOR INTEGRATING THE CURRICULUM

The American public has charged educators at all levels with the task of school improvement. Opinion polls and national studies call for educational change and accountability. In this latest reform era, teachers must produce measurable outcomes in student achievement and attitude development.

Teachers, however, wrestle contradictions as they attempt to meet these charges. Children need to show measurable learning gains in achievement, skills, and attitudes. Yet, evidence suggests that traditional methods of instruction do not readily produce achievement or skill gains, and may actually hinder attitudinal growth. Major reform of the ways in which schools treat children may be necessary to produce significant learning gains. Yet, public opinion and financial resources limit the extent to which change can occur.

Fortunately, a teaching strategy exists that shows promise for resolving these contradictions. Multidisciplinary teaching approaches that merge traditional content areas have potential to produce gains in student achievement, skill acquisition and, most importantly, attitude development. These integrative activities, moreover, can be accomplished within the limits of school structure and current school budgets.

THE SOCIAL STUDIES-CHILDREN'S FICTION CONNECTION

In this book, we explore perhaps the most promising of these multidisciplinary strategies, integrating children's literature and social studies instruction. We use the term "children's literature" to mean storybooks, picture books, and books of verse — only fiction. By social studies instruction, we mean teaching children the knowledge, skills, and attitudes needed for effective citizenship. Such citizenship teaching, in our view, is preparing children to make effective decisions about society's future welfare.

In this integrative stategy, we link social studies and children's literature in tandem. Teachers use the characters, plot, settings, themes, and relationships in selected story and picture books to develop activities that promote social studies learning. Creative teachers have found that picture books sug-

gest a range of social studies activities and also provide much of their content. For the resourceful teacher, connecting children's fiction and social studies teaching offers tremendous possibilities!

WHY CHILDREN'S LITERATURE AND SOCIAL STUDIES?

Admittedly, children's literature and social studies teaching seems something of an "odd couple." Picture books seem whimsical, fanciful creations without purpose or deeper meaning. Teaching social decision making, by contrast, seems academic and serious with real implications for individual growth and the common good.

After some thought, though, pairing social studies teaching and children's fiction makes great sense, particularly in the primary grades. Young children build citizenship qualities in order to function in adult society. To contribute to social welfare, youngsters learn lessons about the ways in which people live. They acquire skills to become effective social decision makers and develop the commitment to participate in the decision-making process.

Opportunities for children to model these citizenship qualities fill the pages of story and picture books. These works contain knowledge about people from many backgrounds and different time periods. Characters deal with emerging values, demonstrate the effect of institutions on individual behavior, and relate with others in many situations.

Finally, storybooks provide examples of citizenship skills being practiced. Characters communicate with others, determine cause / effect relationships, locate places on maps, process information, and think reflectively. They are concerned about and involved in their society. Characters confront choices every citizen must make, and circumstances force them to make decisions that influence the welfare of others. Far from a mismatch, social studies teaching and children's fiction seem a dynamic duo!

THE DESIGN AND STRUCTURE OF THE BOOK

This activity book contains twenty chapters. Each chapter describes social studies activities suggested by a work of children's fiction. These twenty children's books were selected for their literary quality, appeal to children, and potential contributions to social studies teaching.

Selecting Quality Books

Perhaps the most crucial aspect of using children's fiction to teach social studies is the selection of quality books. Quality books tend to avoid the sterotyping and misinformation that is fatal to effective social studies teaching. Quality fiction, moreover, confronts themes and issues that future citizens should encounter.

With the importance of selecting quality books in mind, we checked various references before finalizing our twenty choices. For literary quality, we consulted the Newbery and Caldecott Award lists as well as several American Library Association (ALA) publications. We also referenced children's preference lists (including Nebraska's Golden Sower Award and the International Reading Association / Children's Book Council's "Children's Choices") to find quality books with relevance and appeal for children. For potential social studies value, we examined "Notable Children's Trade Books in the Field of Social Studies," a bibliography published yearly by the National Council for the Social Studies (NCSS).

The annotated bibliography at the end of this book contains complete information about these references as well as other sources helpful for integrating social studies and children's fiction.

Reading Levels Provided

Besides using quality books with social studies value and appeal for children, we have tried to include books with appropriate readability levels for primary children. This task is not as easy as it might seem as picture books are typically less readable than they first appear. For each grade level, we chose books that beginning readers might realistically tackle as well as some books that demand teacher assistance. The readability level for each selection is given on the title page of each chapter. These levels were computed using the Spache and Fry scales (perhaps the most practical of the many formulas now available).

Selections Grouped by Grade Level

The book's twenty chapters are grouped into four sections by grade level, K-3. Each section contains five books that share a common theme appropriate for a primary grade level. Additional books appropriate for each grade level are listed in the bibliography, "More Children's Books", located in

the appendices. We "borrowed" the grade level themes from the social studies curriculum pattern typically followed by textbook editors (the "Expanding Environments" approach developed some forty years ago). Each theme, in other words, parallels the major focus of the "Expanding Environments" curriculum for that particular grade level.

However, these may be selected at any grade level if the teacher wishes to integrate the skills emphasized with her / his objective for any compatible lesson. The sections and themes are listed below.

> Section I: "Understanding the Self" (Kindergarten)
>
> Section II: "Living Together in Families" (Grade One)
>
> Section III: "Discovering the Neighborhood" (Grade Two)
>
> Section IV: "Learning about Communities" (Grade Three)

DELIVERING THE BOOKS TO CHILDREN

Sitting down individually and reading a book quietly seems the most advantageous means for children to discover any story. Yet, many works presented in this activity book are simply too difficult for primary youngsters to read alone. School libraries, moreover, do not contain multiple copies of many of these twenty books. Consequently, we have devised several ways of delivering these stories to young readers.

First of all, a single copy can be shared with an entire class or large group of students in the following ways.

a. The teacher reads the book to students as part of a "reading time"

b. Selected students take turns reading the book aloud to the class.

c. The teacher uses an opaque projector so that students can read passages of the book silently.

Secondly, small groups of students may share limited copies of a picture book as follows.

a. Students in a small group may read aloud to each other, apart from the regular classroom where other teaching may be occurring.

b. Copies may be assigned to teams of

two or three students; team members then arrange to share the book (including overnight sharing) until all have read the book.

   c. The book may be placed in classroom "reserve" for borrowing by teams of readers.

Thirdly, an individual student may read the book in a number of ways.

   a. The student reads the book and summarizes it for a small or large group of peers.

   b. A student presents a synopsis of the book to the teacher; the teacher then expands this summary for the entire class.

Additionally, a book may be delivered to young readers in more creative fashions. These modes of presentation increase children's enthusiasm as well as adding an "arts dimension" to the story:

   a. A group of 2-3 children may present a "reader's theater" dramatization of a selection.

   b. A small group may role play an excerpt from a story using either paraphrasing or exact dialogue.

   c. An overhead projector "shadow play" of a passage or two boosts student interest and increases understanding of key ideas in the story.

CHAPTER ORGANIZATION

Every chapter begins with a complete bibliographic entry for a children's book, the book's readability level, and a plot summary. An explanation of specific ways in which this book might be integrated with social studies teaching follows this introductory information.

The bulk of each chapter is devoted to social studies activities suggested by a story or picture book. These activities are presented in five categories; the categories parallel skill areas generally found in social studies programs at the primary level.

1. Developing Communication Skills. The ability to communicate orally and in writing are essentials for good citizenship.
2. Nurturing the Affective Domain. This "skill area" furthers the empathetic, personal dimension of social decision making; elements of this area include: self-concept, self-awareness, seeing other viewpoints, and multicultural understanding.
3. Promoting Thinking skills. Reflective thinking is a hallmark of "good" citizenship. Subskills of reflective thinking include: sequencing, classifying, comparing / contrasting, predicting, inferring and problem solving.
4. Using Map and Globe Skills. Spatial awareness is a key to effective social decision making. Activities in this category encourage practical application of the tools of geography.
5. Practicing Social Interaction. Citizenship cannot be practiced without exchanging ideas and relating to others. These activities allow students to interact in small and large group settings.

We must note that these divisions will seem arbitrary at times; many activities build a variety of these skill areas and resist labeling with a specific category. These divisions are more an organizational convenience than an attempt to limit the possible uses of a particular activity.

CHAPTER ACTIVITIES

Every activity in this book reflects our firm belief that the knowledge, skills, and attitudes of citizenship can only be learned by doing. Activities are "hands-on," interactive, investigative experiences in which children can model citizenship qualities in familiar settings. These activities let children "do something" with social studies content and apply social studies skills. While the activities are best suited for small and large groups of students, many can be adapted for use with individuals.

Activities, moreover, are not necessarily dependent on a particular story or picture book. The creative teacher might find an activity recommended for one selection that would work perfectly well with other books. We encourage teachers to experiment and adapt activities to help make learning by students both interesting and educational.

CHAPTER ONE

Bear's Picture
by Daniel Pinkwater

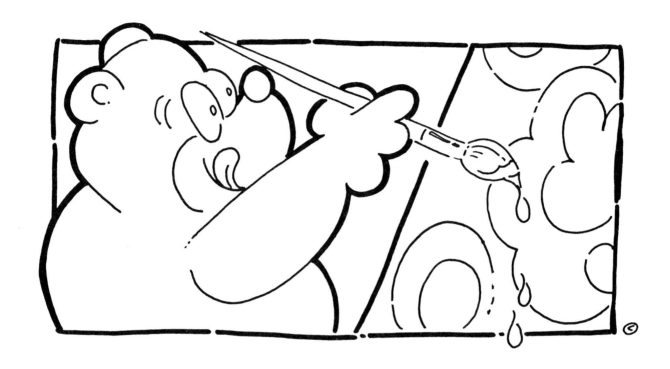

An IRA/CBC "Children's Choices" selection for 1985

Spache Readability Level—4+
Fry Readability Level—2

Pinkwater, Daniel. ***Bear's Picture***. New York: E.P. Dutton, 1984. Unpaged (approx. 36 pages). ISBN 0-525-44102-6.

   Pinkwater weaves a fanciful yarn about a bear's struggle to express himself despite the comments of self-appointed critics. As Bear paints a wildly colorful picture, two fine, proper gentlemen approach. They inform Bear that his art makes no sense and, besides, bears really shouldn't be painting pictures anyway. Bear says simply that the painting can be anything he wants it to be because it is his. As the gentlemen walk off, they launch a parting criticism of Bear's work. Ignoring them, Bear looks at his painting and feels happy inside.

Relationship to Social Studies

Pinkwater's book is a natural addition to kindergarten social studies programs emphasizing self-awareness, self-concept, and self-direction. Bear's story is a forceful argument for individuality and the right of self-expression. In our sometimes homogenized and conformist society, children need exposure to individuals like Bear who refuse to be always bound by establishment conventions. While Pinkwater may not stress individualism's responsibilities as much as its rights, a teacher can correct this imbalance easily enough.

Bear's Picture also suggests several activities that build children's ability to think creatively and analyze information. The book also introduces a number of opportunities to boost students' communication skills—both oral and symbolic.

Like *Pamela Camel*, Pinkwater's work is not nearly as "readable" as it might seem at first glance. The vocabulary is complex and difficult for young children to understand. The book, therefore, should be read aloud with appropriate pre- and post-reading experiences to aid comprehension.

Developing Communication Skills

Pinkwater's story provides many chances to show children that people are unique individuals who often communicate similar ideas very differently. Two of these opportunities are described below.

1. Read the story aloud; in a follow-up discussion, leave children with the notion that Bear chose subjects for his artwork (a honey tree, hollow log, etc.) that he knew well and painted them in a very personal way. Bear's familiarity with his subjects at least partly explains his confidence in and happiness with his work. Provide children with art supplies (the more imaginative the materials the better); allow them to create a very personal vision of something that they know very well and love very much. Let children share their art if they like.

2. After reading the story to children, discuss the fact that Bear's conception of familiar forest settings was very different than the views of two fine, proper gentlemen. With children's input, choose one of the scenes Bear tried to capture in his painting (hopefully, one that children are familiar with; substitute another subject if forest scenes are alien your youngsters). Then, have each child draw a picture of this subject using marking pens and acetate.

Provide time for children to share their pictures on an overhead projector. Discuss with children the different ways in which they depicted the same thing; leave children with the idea that these differences are legitimate results of their uniqueness and individuality. Also point out to children the common elements that their drawings share—features that enable viewers to grasp the meaning conveyed in each picture.

Nurturing the Affective Domain

Bear's Picture raises a number of values issues that young children need to begin considering as part of their preparation for citizenship. After reading the book aloud, the following topics should generate lively and productive discussion for a small group or an entire class.

1. Reread the passage in which the "two fine, proper gentlemen" first meet Bear. Ask children what the word, "gentleman," means. Ask children how the two "gentlemen" in this story behave. Discuss whether or not these characters were really "gentlemen." Conclude discussion by generating a list of behaviors that a "gentleman" demonstrates.

2. Read passages in which the two gentlemen criticize and ultimately dismiss Bear's artwork. Discuss with children whether or not a person should poke fun at the work (or clothes, or speech, or appearance) of other people. Guide children to two related observations: criticism; constructive criticism that helps someone is far better than negative criticism that only hurts feelings.

Promoting Thinking Skills

The book suggests experiences in which children speculate and analyze content from the story. The following activities represent a sample of the many thinking-skill activities that Pinkwater's work might introduce.

1. Read the story aloud, then focus a brief discussion on the passage in which the two gentlemen guess the meaning of Bear's picture. Review these guesses with children. Show children the illustration of Bear's completed work (the last page of text). Use the following questions to prompt an analysis of the gentlemen's guesswork.

a. Do you think the two gentlemen made good guesses? Why? Why not?

b. What do you think Bear's picture means? Show me on Bear's picture why you think it means that.

2. Read the book aloud, then briefly review the main events of the story with children. Direct children's attention to the story's title character. Use the questions below to generate a class discussion of Pinkwater's use of a bear as the focal point for his story.

a. Tell me about Bear. What does he look like? How does he act? Do you like Bear? Why? Why not?

b. What other animals might the author have used? Why?

c. Would you use an animal or a person as the main character? Why? If an animal, which animal? Why?

Using Map and Globe Skills

Pinkwater's story introduces two activities that build students' readiness for more involved geographic skill-building in later grades.

1. Read the story aloud, then reread two passages: the first appearance of the two gentlemen and their exit from the story. Explain to children that the author tells us little about where the gentlemen had been before they met Bear or where they were going after they left him. Speculate with children about where the gentlemen came from and where they were headed. To extend the activity, children can draw pictures of these places and share their efforts with the class.

2. Read the story to students, then focus on Bear's explanation of the meaning of his painting. Show children drawings you have made (or photos you have taken; or pictures cut from magazines) of the five settings Bear tried to capture. Have volunteers arrange these visuals on a flannel board (or wall, or chalkboard, or the floor) to create a "map" of the forest in which Bear lived. Develop alternate "maps" of Bear's home. Briefly discuss maps and map-making to conclude the activity.

Practicing Social Interaction Skills

Many of the above activities can be adjusted to include small group interaction and participation. Additionally, the following activity allows children to practice cooperation and their ability to interact productively in a group setting.

Read the story to students and then review the sequence in which Bear created his "masterpiece" (an orange squiggle, some blue, a rainbow, green splotches, yellow, and purple parts). Divide children into small groups (6 in each group). Provide each group with a large sheet of newsprint, one big brush, and the colors Bear used in his painting. In each group, have students take turns and recreate the sequence that Bear followed. When all groups have completed their paintings, provide sharing time, being careful **not** to compare the results with Bear's effort.

CHAPTER TWO

Pamela Camel
by Bill Peet

The International Reading Association/Children's Book Council named this book a "Children's Choice" for 1985.

Spache Readability Level—7

Peet, Bill. **Pamela Camel.** Boston: Houghton Mifflin, 1984. 30 pages. ISBN 0-395-35975-9.

Peet spins the tale of a camel's rise from menagerie outcast to star attraction in the Brinkerhoff Brothers Big Top Circus. Audiences laughed at Pamela Camel; they called her names, such as, "stupid brute" because she could not do clever tricks. Very depressed, Pamela broke her tether rope and tiptoed out of the circus yard one afternoon. She followed the surest route to a better life, the nearby railroad tracks.

Soon she came upon a broken rail. Pamela knew this damage meant a certain train wreck. While wanting to report the break, a sudden storm shook her resolve (Pamela was terrified of storms). After hiding for a time, Pamela heard the sounds of an approaching train. In spite of her fear, she stood bravely on the tracks, facing the onrushing locomotive. The engineer braked the train to a halt inches from the broken rail and Pamela.

Realizing what she had done, the engineer proclaimed her a heroine; her owners soon agreed. Pamela returned to the circus, not to the menagerie, but to top-billing as the "Most Amazing and Extraordinary Dromedary Ever to Walk the Face of the Earth!" No one ever called Pamela "stupid" again.

Relationship to Social Studies

For any kindergarten social studies program geared to exploring the "Self," *Pamela Camel* can be a valuable resource. The book's main character confronts many disturbing emotions (fear, embarrassment, etc.); her example might help young children deal with similar feelings they are only beginning to understand. Pamela also faces and ultimately overcomes stereotyping and prejudice (circus audiences label her "dumb" because she is a camel and, therefore, cantankerous and stupid). Children need to learn the lesson that individuals are much more than they appear on the surface.

The book also suggests a number of activities that promote children's thinking skills (principally their ability to categorize and to reference a time period different than their immediate present). Pamela's dash from her circus confines might provide content for introductory map and globe activities as well.

Obviously, the book's lengthy text necessitates reading it aloud to a large group of young children. The vocabulary and involved plot, moreover, boost comprehension beyond a level that many kindergarteners can understand without assistance. Pre-reading explanations and post-reading discussion will be needed for youngsters to fully grasp the story.

Developing Communication Skills

Peet tells a complex and witty story about the resolution of a camel's identity crisis. Retelling this saga and creating variations on it can afford young children the opportunity to build important oral and written communication skills.

1. Read the story aloud to the class and discuss it briefly, being sure than students establish a chronology of major events. Next, divide students into pairs, naming one child in each pair the "teller" and one the "listener." Have the "tellers" summarize Pamela's story for the "listeners;" then, let students switch roles before the story is retold a second time. Encourage students to compare the versions of Peet's tale that they heard and the ones they told. Use the following questions to stimulate this discussion:

a. How were they similar?
b. How were they different?
c. Why these differences?
d. If two people retold a story, would their versions always be different? Why? Why not?

2. Read the story aloud and establish a chronology of its major events with students. Then, ask what other animals might live in a circus (the illustration on pp.4-5 might refresh memories). Speculate with children how Peet's story might change if the main character was one of these other animals instead of a camel. Give students some "thinking time" to select a circus animal (other than a camel) and create a new version of Peet's book with this animal as the main character. Remind students that their story would, among other things, need a different title than Peet's (perhaps *Eleanor Elephant?*.

Use the language experience approach to record these stories in written form (i.e. children dictate their stories to a parent, aide, or older student who writes them on paper). When all stories have been transcribed and edited, children may "read" their stories to the class. An alternative to the experience story is to have children draw a picture of an event in the "new" story.

Nurturing the Affective Domain

Pamela Camel offers children opportunities to explore emotions that they possibly share with Pamela. The activities listed below encourage this exploration of personal feelings.

1. Read the story aloud and discuss it with students, focusing on Pamels's encounter with the thunderstorm (pp.23-14). Leave students with the conclusion that this storm badly frightened Pamela. Remind children that everyone is afraid of something; share something that scares you and then ask children to share their fears (be sure to call only on volunteers during this discussion).

Then, have children, working individually, draw a picture of something that scares them (as a variation, have children cut examples of this scary thing from newspapers or magazines and paste them on colored paper). Bring the class back together; al-

6

low volunteers to share their pictures. To conclude the activity, place a wastebasket in the center of the group; have students, one-by-one, dispose of their fears in the trash.

2. As a follow-up to the first activity, ask children if fears are always this easy to eliminate. Can all fears just be thrown away? Discuss other ways that children can dispose of even their most nagging frights (i.e. talk them over with parents, tackle them "head-on," etc.).

Promoting Thinking Skills

After reading the book to students, consider the following activities designed to build their ability to categorize and to distinguish the past from the present.

1. Seat children in a circle on the floor. In the center of the circle, place two pieces of construction paper—one marked "Yes" and the other "No". Remind children that Pamela was a circus animal; tell children that you want them to find other animals that could be circus animals. Show children photos of many "animals" (be liberal in your definition of "animal;" include birds, fish, reptiles, etc.); for each example, ask individual children, "Is this a circus animal?" (be liberal in your definition of "animal;" include birds, fish, reptiles, etc.); for each example, ask individual children, "Is this a circus animal?" Have the children respond by placing the photo on the "Yes" sheet or the "No" sheet.

After all examples have been categorized, ask students what qualities the "Yes" animals share that make them circus animals; write these qualities on the board. Ask the people what elements the "No" animals have that prevent them from being circus animals. Go back through each pile and have students check the accuracy of their decisions based on these characteristics. Review the attributes of circus animals with students.

2. To extend the first activity, have children develop subgroups for the "Yes" animals (i.e. "animals that pull circus wagons," "animals that perform," etc.) and the "No" animals (i.e. "pets," "wild animals," etc.). Discuss attributes for each of these new categories with students.

3. Focus on Peet's description of the setting for *Pamela Camel*, particularly his statement that the

story happened "a long time ago" (p. 1). Show students selected illustrations from the book (particularly the one on p. 27); ask children to pinpoint out evidence from the pictures that show that the story did indeed happen "a long time ago." Ask them to list ways in which the pictures would differ if the story happened now.

Have children observe their classroom and describe how it differs from a classroom that existed when Pamela's story occurred. Further, have children give examples of events that happened or people who lived "a long time ago" and tell how they differ from events and people today (a note of caution—do not be offended when students inevitably include you among the relics of "a long time ago!"

Using Map and Globe Skills

Peet's work suggests a number of simple activities that will increase children's readiness for more involved map and globe skill-building lessons in later grades.

1. Read the book aloud and summarize its plot with students. Quickly focus this discussion on the setting, the Brinkerhoff Brothers Big Top Circus a long time ago. Have students name major elements of the circus and speculate about what they looked like. Provide students with a map outline of a three-ring circus like the one shown at the end of the chapter.

Briefly explain what maps are and why people make them. Then, have students locate the major elements of the circus on their map cutlines. After everyone has finished, encourage students to share their "maps" with the class. Conclude with a quick review of the "what and why" of maps.

2. Read the story aloud and review its main events with students. Place particular emphasis on the landmarks Pamela encountered on her travels. Then seat students on the floor in a large circle. Tell them that they will build a "map" to show Pamela's journey. Call on individual students to place models of each place Pamela visited in an appropriate location in the center of the circle; these models can be very simple outlines cut from paper; be sure that children locate the models in correct relationship to each other, but do not try for technical precision in the scale of this "map." If time

allows, have children use a toy camel (or horse) to show the route Pamela took from place to place. To conclude this activity, discuss how this "map" differs from the maps children have seen parents use on family trips; discuss how it is similar.

Practicing Social Interaction Skills

Pamela Camel suggests several small group tasks and larger group experiences that afford students opportunity to interact with each other.

1. After reading the story to students, discuss the grand procession into the big top that ends Pamela's tale. Plan a "grand procession" through the school and/or library; help students determine the types of animals that would march in a circus parade.

Then, have students work in small groups (up to 3 students each) to decorate animal heads made from shopping bags.

Use crayons, colored construction paper, and bits of cast-off materials. Fill the bags with newspaper and tie off the opening with string. Children hold the animal heads in front of them.

This work time might continue for one of two periods. When everyone has finished, order your marchers and let the procession begin!

2. Read the story aloud; focus a follow-up discussion on the abuse Pamela received from circus audiences. Guide children to the conclusion that these labels were not polite to use nor correct in describing Pamela.

Discuss how these insults made Pamela feel; discuss how they might make children feel. Divide children into small groups (about 3 students each); have each group brainstorm things they might say to Pamela to make her feel better about herself. Allow each group to share results. Conclude with a review of the way in which Pamela showed her true character and changed people's opinions about her.

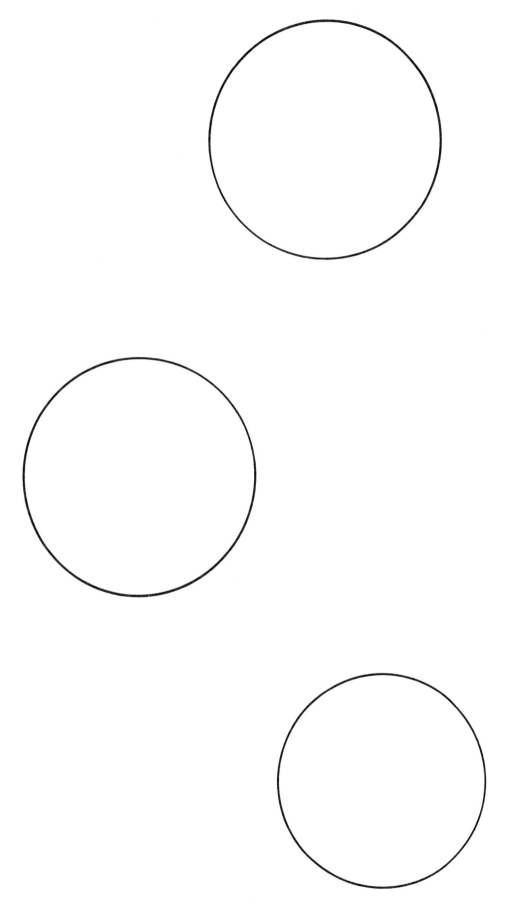

THE BRINKERHOFF BROTHERS BIG TOP CIRCUS TENT

CHAPTER THREE
Her Majesty, Aunt Essie
by Amy Schwartz

Selected for the IRA/CBC's "Children's Choices" list in 1985.

Spache Readability Level—4 +
Fry Readability Level—4

Schwartz, Amy. **Her Majesty, Aunt Essie.** Scarsdale, NY: Bradbury Press, 1984. Unpaged (approx. 26 pages). ISBN 0-02-781450-5.

Schwartz delights readers with this tale of a small girl's quest to convince a skeptical friend of her relation to royalty. Aunt Essie moves in with Ruthie's family and, from first arrival, Ruthie **knows** that her aunt is a queen. After all, Aunt Essie acts with the self-centeredness and down-right arrogance that only a queen would display. Ruthie boasts of her lineage to her friend, Maisie, who only laughs. Outraged, Ruthie wagers the family dog, Joe, that she can prove to Maisie by midnight that Aunt Essie is a royal person. By early evening, Ruthie despairs that the bet is lost—she has tried everything and Maisie remains doubtful. In the nick of time, Aunt Essie's grand departure for a dinner date convinces Maisie that royal blood flows in Ruthie's veins after all.

Relationship to Social Studies

Among its many social studies possibilities, Schwartz's book has a multicultural dimension that young children should experinece. Ruthie's ethnic background and lifestyle (urban Jewish) are not ones that most children view every day. Schwartz sets her tale in a place (Booklyn) and a time (the 1950's) that should also broaden the horizons of most youngsters.

The book, moveover, has a strong affective dimension as it deals realistically with a small girl's aspirations, emotions, and beliefs. Schwartz's book might also introduce map and globe or social interaction skill-building activities.

Schwartz adopts a child's perspective in chronicling Ruthie's struggle to prove a fervent belief to a doubting friend. Children should find the main characters' maneuverings familiar, comical, and most interesting. The book's appeal should add tremendous impact to its many social studies lessons.

While interesting and believable for primary children, the book is not independently accessible for them. The setting, involved story line, and high readability level make reading-aloud the most effective way to deliver this story to students. Pre-reading exercises and post-reading discussion should accompany the read-aloud session to ensure comprehension.

Developing Communication Skills

Schwartz's fascinating characters communicate in various ways as the story's plot unfolds. Consequently, the book suggests several activities in which children investigate these modes of communication.

1. Read the story to children and briefly discuss its main events. Focus discussion on the passage in which Aunt Essie talked with Mrs. Katz on the telephone. Divide children into pairs. Have them take turns role playing a phone conversation in which they communicate a "vitally important message" to a concerned listener. These conversations can be excellent vehicles for reinforcing stu-

dents' good telephone manners (both "talking" and "listening" manners).

2. Read the story to children and establish a chronology of events. Next reread passages in which Aunt Essie nonverbally communicates her "royalty" to Ruthie (particularly the final scene in which Aunt Essie emerges from Ruthie's house). Use Aunt Essie's example to review essential features of nonverbal communication with children (hand-gestures, facial expressions, movement, clothing, etc.). Then, allow children to choose an occupation or animal that interests them and pantomime it for the class. Conclude the activity by asking the class to guess the occupation/animal that each child communicates.

Nurturing the Affective Domain

Schwartz's story can be a wonderfully effective vehicle for helping children explore their own emerging feelings and values. Opportunities for such exploration include the following activities.

1. Read the story aloud and discuss Aunt Essie's personality with children. Ask them why she seemed so much like a queen to Ruthie. Guide children the observation that her most "queen-like" quality was her almost limitless self-confidence; Aunt Essie felt so good about herself that she seemed like royalty.

2. Give children the opportunity to be "kings" and "queens" for a day in your classroom. Provide materials for them to make crowns and wear them for an entire class session (morning, afternoon, or all day). Use this time to reinforce children's self-concepts and build their self-confidence to "royal" proportions.

Promoting Thinking Skills

Her Majesty, Aunt Essie contains a variety of plot elements that children can classify and categorize. The characters also make decisions that children can analyze. Read the book aloud and then consider using the following activities that let children practice these thinking skills.

1. First, let children generate a list of all the

things that make Aunt Essie seem like a queen (the picture of the mustachioed man, the dangling earrings, her tea drinking, giving orders, etc.). Provide children with three simple categories: "Similar" (from what we would see around our town); and "Different" (from things we see in our town). Have children place items from the picture in the appropriate category. Ask children to justify their choices; if possible, have children come to consensus regarding their placements.

Using Map and Globe Skills

Her Majesty, Aunt Essie exposes readers to several places and cultures that might be quite different from the one they experience daily. Consequently, consider using the book to introduce activities in which your students study these varied places and peoples.

For all of these activities, read Schwartz's story aloud, briefly discuss the author's reference to the place you have chosen, and then adopt the "immersion" approach to examine this place/culture in depth. In the "immersion" approach, children are literally plunged into the daily life of a locale as much as possible. Let children experience the physical location, climate, architecture, art, music, dance, folk tales, food, games, and language of a culture different from their own; in short, immerse them in a way of life they might not otherwise know. Follow these immersion experiences with a discussion session in which children list ways in which this place/culture is similar to their way of life and ways in which it differs. Places/cultures suggested by Schwartz's picture book include:

a. New York City (the story is set in Brooklyn)
b. France (note that Aunt Essie speaks French to Mrs. Katz)
c. Judaism (Ruthie's family belonged to this religious/cultural group)
d. Israel (a Jewish nation)
e. Great Britain (or any other country with a king or queen)
f. the closest "Big City" (the story reflects an urban lifestyle)

Practicing Social Interaction Skills

Schwartz's story suggests many opportunities for children to hone their ability to interact productively, including the following activities.

1. Read the book aloud, then discuss the ways in which the two friends, Ruthie and Maisie, "get along." Generate a list of descriptors for their relationship (i.e. "loyal to each other," "sometimes fight," "love each other," etc.). Also, discuss how they resolve the conflicts that inevitably arise in any friendship. Finally, develop a list of "rules" for keeping a friendship happy and productive.

2. Read the book aloud, then focus discussion on the family tree that Ruthie draws and shares with Maisie. Explain a "family tree" to students in simplified form (a diagram that shows members of your immediate family). Have students construct a family tree. They can either draw one freehand like Ruthie or complete a family tree worksheet like the one shown here.

After family trees are finished, students may share them with the class. A note of caution needs to be sounded at this point. In today's world of "broken" and non-traditional family structures, fmaily trees may be quite varied. Tell children that there are different kinds of families and, therefore, family trees will look different from one person to another.

Inform the parents of the upcoming project. Request that they supply information concerning grandparents' names, parents' names, and sibling names. Make a place on the paper for parent(s) to sign indicating that making the family tree is agreed to. Use this imformation to help the child understand his/her family tree.

OUR FAMILY TREE

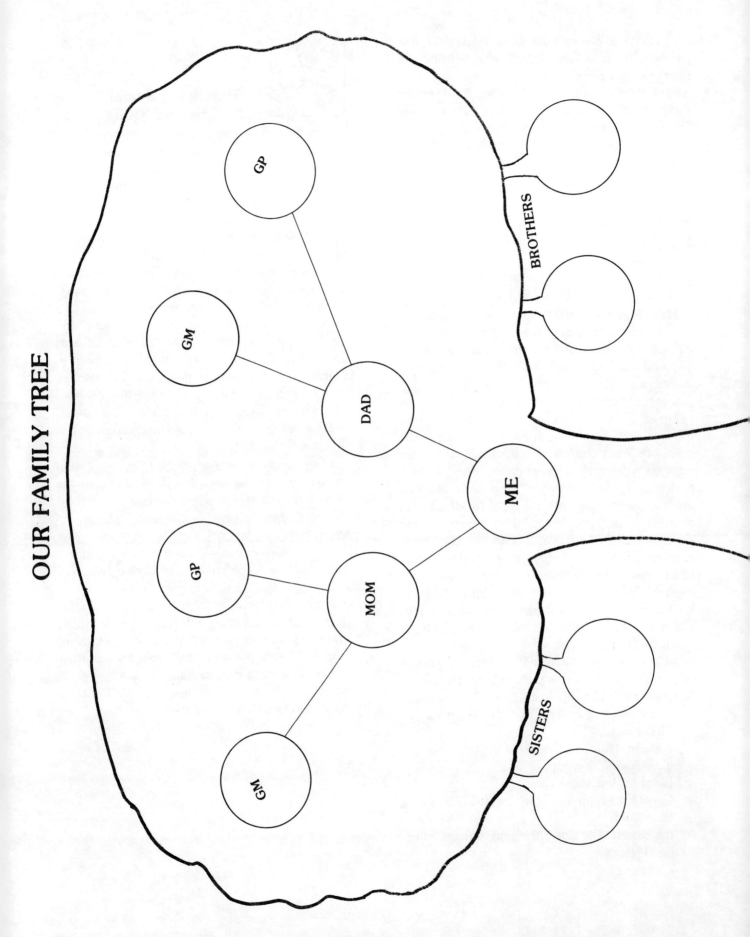

CHAPTER FOUR

My Mama Needs Me
by Mildred Pitts Walter

Winner of the Coretta Scott King Award for Illustrations, 1984; nominated for the Golden Sower Award (Nebraska), 1984; included with the National Council for the Social Studies' "Notable Trade Books in the Field of Social Studies," 1983.

Spache Readability Level—4 +
Fry Readability Level—1

Walter, Mildred Pitts. **My Mama Needs Me**. Pictures by Pat Cummings. New York: Lothrop, Lee, and Shepard, 1983. Unpaged (approx. 32 pages). ISBN 0-688-01671-5.

Walter's realistic, yet tenderly told story, deals with a difficult experience for many young children—the accomodation of a newborn into family routines. Like most youngsters, Jason feels love, pride and responsibility for the sister newly arrived from the hospital. As her first day at home draws on, however, Jason also begins to feel rejected, a little hurt, protective, and just plain bored as he waits for his sister to do something beyond eat, sleep, and cry. After awhile, Mama shows Jason that he not only can help care for his sister, but should play with friends and be himself as well.

Relationship to Social Studies

Mildred Pitts Walter has written a book that directly relates to the primary thrust of kindergarten social studies programs. Instructions at this level emphasizes self-study, self-awareness, and self-concept. In a sensitive manner, *My Mama Needs Me* reveals the feelings that many children face when a new brother or sister comes home for the first time. The book fosters children's understanding of a key time in their lives and augments their feelings of self-worth. In a very real sense, the book shares the major purpose for early children social studies teaching.

Additionally, Walter's work adds an important multicultural dimension to kindergarten social studies. Jason's family is Black and lives in a multi-ethnic neighborhood where people of several races constructively interact. Jason's example, moreover, negates many stereotypes that persist about the "typical" Black family. Jason's mother is an informed and caring parent; his father works to support a comfortable lifestyle for his loved ones. In today's increasingly pluralistic society, children badly need exposure to positive multicultural role models similar to Jason's family.

As with other kindergarten titles we have selected, *My Mama Needs Me* is best read aloud to a large group of students. Because of some unfamiliar vocabulary and sensitive subject matter, the book should be introduced carefully before reading and discussed thoroughly afterwards.

Developing Communication Skills

Walter's story presents opportunities for children to investigate the varied ways in which people communicate their thoughts and feelings. Read the book aloud and then consider implementing one of the following activities that examine aspects of communication.

1. Generate a list of times in which Jason communicated with other characters (Jason and his friends, Mama and Jason, Jason and the sleeping baby, Jason and Mrs. Luby, etc.). Use the following questions to discuss several of these interac-

tions with children.
 a. What did these people communicate to Jason?
 b. Did they always communicate by "telling" Jason?
 c. What are some other ways in which they communicated their ideas?
 d. Do you ever communicate in ways other than "telling?"

2. Discuss the story's conclusion with students. Focus on Mama's message to Jason that she really loved and needed him. Ask children to describe how she communicated this message to her son. Ask children how their mothers, fathers, or guardians communicate this message to them.

Nurturing the Affective Domain

The following activities explore emotions that many young chldren have felt or may one day experience.

1. After reading the book aloud, discuss Jason's feelings for his new sister with a large group of students. Ask children if they have a brother or sister (or cousin or special friend for "only-children") that makes them feel the same way. Provide time for children to share these feelings with the group. To extend this activity, children may draw a picture of this special person and share it with the class.

2. Read the story aloud and discuss Jason's relationships with his many friends (Mrs. Luby, Mr. Pompey, Craig, Terry, etc.). Play recordings or sing several happy, upbeat songs. Have children match each friendship that Jason enjoys with the song that best "describes" that relationship. Appropriate songs may be found on recordings by Ella Jenkins, Hap Palmer, and Raffi.

Developing Thinking Skills

In this story, Jason chooses between his "duty" to his sister and playing with friends several times. These choices suggest activities in which children must weigh alternatives and make a decision. Two such lessons are described below.

1. Read the story aloud then focus discussion on a passage in which Jason decides to leave friends in order to be with his sister (his meetings with Mrs. Luby and Mr. Pompey are probably your best possibilities). In a "give-and-take" with children, guide them through the following process for analyzing Jason's decision.

    a. What was Jason doing with his friend?

    b. Why did he decide to leave his friend?

    c. What happened as a result of his decision to leave?

    d. Was his decision a good one? Why? Why not?

    e. What else might Jason have done?

    f. What would you have done if you were in Jason's shoes?

2. Using the process outlined above, guide children through an analysis of a decision that a member of the class has made recently. You might also use a decision that you made that has influenced students in some way (i.e. the decision not to go out for recess).

Using Map and Globe Skills

To promote children's understanding of what maps are and why we make them, have children make a simple "map" of the pond that Jason and Mr. Pompey visited. "Maps" need not be precisely drawn to scale—in fact, they will probably resemble drawings much more than advanced cartography. The important thing is not technical precision, but giving children a chance to represent a location on paper and to begin grasping basic features that maps demonstrate.

Reproduce a rough outline of the pond on a handout; let children sketch as many details on their outlines as they can (ducks, plants, people, the bridge, paths, bushes, rocks, cattails, etc.); display their efforts when they are done (or provide a sharing session if time permits). This activity can be replicated with other locations described in the story (a room in Jason's house, the route Jason and Mr. Pompey walked, Mrs. Luby's yard, etc.).

Practicing Social Interaction Skills

When *My Mama Needs Me* has been read to children, consider using any of the following activities to encourage children's ability to interact with others.

1. Review the major events of the story with children. Guide them to the observation that *My Mama Needs Me* chronicles the main events of a day in a young boy's life. Divide children into small groups (2-3 children per group). Have them dictate a story (either into a tape recorder or to someone who can write it down) that tells the main events of the previous day at school. Let groups share their stories with the class at a later date.

2. Point out to the children that Jason has many friends. Show the picture at the end of the story that shows these friends swinging. Ask children what other things Jason and his buddies do to have fun; then ask students to think about what fun things they do with their friends. Have each child draw a picture of the "funnest" thing they and their friends do. Display these creations on a "Friends Have Fun" bulletin board.

CHAPTER FIVE
Peabody
by Rosemary Wells

A "Children's Choices" selection in 1984, and a Golden Sower Award nominee the following year.

Spache Readability Level—4+
Fry Readability Level—5

Wells, Rosemary. **Peabody.**. New York: E.P. Dutton, 1983. Unpaged (approx. 32 pages). ISBN 0-8037-0004-0 and 0-8037-0005-9 (library binding).

With simple prose and vibrant watercolors, Wells tells a story of love found, lost, then rediscovered. Peabody, Annie's birthday bear, enjoyed benefits that being a "special friend" can bring. Skiing, outdoor adventures, and a seaside vacation gave Peabody many tales with which to dazzle the other toys on Annie's shelf. Most of all, Annie's love for Peabody made him feel "almost real." Then, disaster struck Peabody at his happiest. Annie received a magical birthday present—Rita, a doll who could talk, walk, drink juice, and sing three songs. For an agonizing time, Peabody languished on the toy self, as Rita replaced him in Annie's heart. Annie's younger brother, Robert, rescued Peabody at last by dunking Rita in the bathtub and ruining her electrical gadgetry. Annie remembered Peabody's special qualities—qualities that did not depend on batteries and circuits—and restored him to his role of sidekick and confidant. Back at Annie's side, Peabody's heart danced once again!

Relationship to Social Studies

Wells manages a remarkable feat—mingling elements of fantasy and whimsy with realistic portrayals of sibling relationships and the behaviors that young children demonstrate. This blend of imagination and realism makes the book a valuable resource for kindergarten social studies teaching. The story's imaginative aspects (a personified bear, talking toys) should capture and hold students' interest. Children should then be "easy targets" for the book's believable lessons about friendship, brother-sister relationships, adjusting to new family arrivals, and coping with sometimes painful emotions (such as rejection, jealously, and sadness).

Besides those contributions to the affective education component of social studies, *Peabody* suggests several activities that build children's thinking skills (particularly, time/order sequencing of the seasons and problem solving scenarios). The story also offers opportunities to promote the ability to perceive spatial relationships.

Although a potentially valuable social studies teaching aid, the book is not one that all kindergarten youngsters will readily understand. The story contains many "advanced" words and some possibly difficult abstractions that may need explanation in the course of a read-aloud session. However, as with any book containing high vocabulary, the teacher may adjust the vocabulary to match the children's understanding.

Developing Communication Skills

Wells' characters communicate ideas and emotions in various ways. Their examples introduce many activities in which children can model these modes of communication. After reading the book to children, consider using the following activities.

1. Ask children how Annie communicated to Peabody that she truly loved him (dressed him warmly, put him on the highest shelf, etc.). Next, ask how Annie convinced Peabody that she no longer cared (left him on the shelf, let Rita spoil his birthday party, etc.).

Then, have children describe someone they love as much as Annie loved Peabody. Discuss with children how they might communicate their feelings to this special person.

2. Remind children that Annie, Robert, and Peabody planted a garden of dandelions and pansies. Discuss with children how flowers can be used to communicate feelings in styrofoam cups, using a classroom window ledge as a greenhouse. Later, students may decorate their "flower pots" and give them to a special someone.

Nurturing the Affective Domain

By examining Annie's sometimes competing relationships with Peabody, Robert, and Rita, young children can begin to deal with their own sometimes contradictory feelings for loved ones. After reading the book aloud, use the following topics/questions to generate discussions in which children explore emotions that they often experience, but may not fully understand.

1. Remind children of the passage in which Annie ignored Peabody. Generate a discussion of Annie's actions by asking students:
   a. What did Annie do to Peabody?
   b. How did Annie make Peabody feel?
   c. How would you describe Annie's treatment of Peabody? (Children might say, "she was mean," or "she was cruel.")
   d. Have you ever treated a friend like Annie treated Peabody?
   e. How did your friend feel? How did you feel later?

2. Have children describe Robert's treatment of Annie's talking-walking doll, Rita. To prompt a discussion of Robert's conduct, ask children:
   a. Just what did Robert do to Rita?
   b. Why did he do those things to Annie's doll?
   c. Was it a good or bad thing that Robert did? Why?

Promoting Thinking Skills

The book suggests a great variety of activities in

which children solve problems, analyze characters' actions, and time-order sequence—including the following possibilities:

1. Read the story to students; review the passage in which Annie shelves her old friend, Peabody. Focus particularly on the sentence, "Without Annie's love, Peabody did not feel real." Ask children if Peabody (a teddy bear) could ever "feel real"? Have them defend their positions.

2. After reading the story aloud, reread the passages in which Rita trumpets, "Good morning. I love you!" Ask individual children to decide whether or not Rita really meant what she said and defend their judgments.

3. Read the story and establish a chronology of major events with students. Help them place Annie's birthday in the appropriate season and sequence the remaining seasons as they occur in the story. Then, provide long strips of drawing paper folded in four sections. Have children draw pictures representing the four seasons Peabody encountered on the appropriate sections of the paper.

Using Map and Globe Skills

The activities below promote: (1) children's awareness that every location demonstrates a set of unique characteristics and (2) their ability to perceive spatial relationships. Both outcomes are prerequisites for map and globe skill-building lessons in later grades.

1. Read *Peabody* to children and then review the settings that the author references in the story. Provide art materials (the more "hands-on" the better—consider using finger paints, for example) and ask each student to create a picture of one of these locations. Be sure that all settings are illustrated. To conclude the activity, help children arrange one set of pictures on a flat surface (the floor, a wall, or a bulletin board). While scale and distance need not be observed, be sure that pictures are in proper relationship to each other. Explain to children that they have constructed a "map" of the settings described in the story. To extend the activity, ask children to trace Peabody's travels on their "map."

2. Read the story aloud, then focus discussion on the many adventures that Peabody enjoyed. Generate a list of these experiences. Then, ask children to name places where Peabody might have had them. Some experiences might occur anywhere (planting the garden, for example). For others (like skiing), have children justify their responses.

Practicing Social Interaction

To encourage constructive student interaction, read the story to children and then remind them that Rita sang three songs when Annie turned her key. Brainstorm with children titles of the three songs Rita could sing on command. When the class has reached consensus, divide children into three small groups; assign each group a song title. Have parents, aides, or student volunteers teach the appropriate song to each small group. To conclude the activity, let the small groups serenade the class as Rita might have done.

CHAPTER SIX

Good As New
by Barbara Douglass

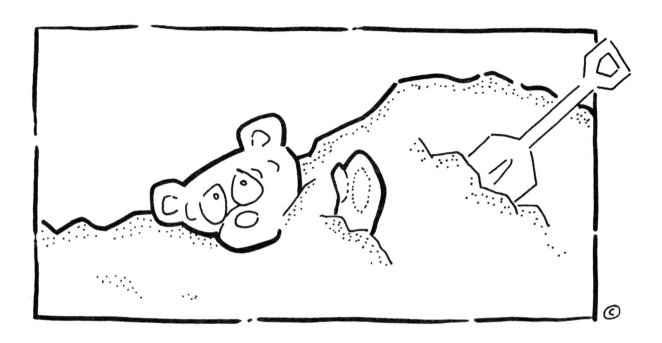

A "Children's Choices" selection of the International Reading Association/Children's Book Council, 1983.

Spache Readability Level—2+

Douglass, Barbara. **Good As New**. Illustrated by Patience Brewster. New York: Lothrop, Lee, and Shepard, 1982. Unpaged (approx. 26 pages). ISBN 0-688-51983-0.

Douglass relates the story of a young boy's emergence from terrible disappointment to happiness as an old "friend" is returned. Grady is crushed after his cousin, K.C., ruins Grady's "most favoritest" thing in the whole world—a stuffed bear. During a visit, K.C. feeds the bear peanut butter, buries it in the sand, and inflicts a variety of "horrors" on the unsuspecting toy till the bear is no longer fit to love. Dad offers to buy a replacement, but Grady just wants his "best buddy" back. Grandpa's assurance, "I can fix that bear," hardly comforts Grady at first. But soon, Grady's pain turns to joy as Grandpa returns his bear to even better than "good as new."

Relationship to Social Studies

Douglass and Brewster create a simple yet powerful story that can strongly support a primary social studies program. First of all, the book contributes to the affective growth of young children in several ways. Grady, for example, models a number of emotions—including distrust, love, anger, frustration, and a sense of loss—with which first graders must learn to deal. Grandpa, moreover, strongly exemplifies values (loyalty, dependability, hard work) that many of today's young children might not otherwise experience. Also, Grandpa shows readers clearly that senior citizens can be valuable individuals, well-worth knowing rather than social outcasts.

Secondly, *Good As New* can introduce various skills of social interaction at a level primary children can readily understand. Grady, for example, is forced by exasperated parents to share a toy he does not want to part with. Grady's parents employ human relations techniques (compromise, conflict resolution, etc.) that any "real life" family uses daily. Additionally, Grady's family (father, mother, Grady, and Grandpa) is not a "typical," nuclear one; in an age of increasingly varied family structures, Grady's situation might afford children opportunity for comparison.

Finally, Grandpa and Grady take a bus ride to buy materials for rebuilding the bear. Their travels provide content for a number of simple activities to build children's map and globe skills.

The book is something of a paradox. Despite its straightforward story line and high interest level for young children, the fairly high readability of *Good As New* makes it difficult for many first graders to read alone. The book is best presented in a "read aloud" or team reading setting.

Developing Communication Skills

After reading the book aloud to a large group of students, consider the following activities to build children's oral communication skills.

1.   Remind students that an otherwise sad story ended on a happy note because Grandpa was able to fix Grady's mistreated bear. Divide students into small groups (4-5 in each group); give each child the opportunity to share a story about a prized possession that someone "brought back to life" or fixed for them.

2.   As a follow-up to the first activity, students may draw a "before" and an "after" picture of the prized possession they described to their small groups. For best results, provide them with manilla drawing paper folded in half length-wise, one side labelled "before" and the other "after."

Nurturing the Affective Domain

The characters in *Good As New* experience feelings that many young children will find familiar. Consequently, the book suggests several activities which might help children better understand their own sometimes confusing emotions.

1.   After reading the story aloud, ask children to describe K.C. Continue until the group agrees on several key descriptions of his character (spoiled, bratty, mean, abandoned, etc.). Then, use the following questions to generate a discussion of K.C. and his relations with other people.

   a. How did K.C. make Grady feel? Why?
   b. How would K.C. make you feel? Why?
   c. Have you ever known someone like K.C.? How did that person make you feel? Describe that experience.
   d. Have you ever acted like K.C.? Even for a little while? How did people around you feel when you did?

2.   Focus on the character of Grandpa. Have children describe Grandpa. Discuss what Grandpa did to make Grady feel so much better. Discuss why Grandpa took the time to fix Grady's bear. Ask if children have ever known someone like Grandpa. Have volunteers share their special someone with the group. As a follow-up activity, have children role play/dramatize this special someone so that the class can "meet" him or her.

Promoting Thinking Skills

After reading the book aloud to a large group of students, the following activities can be used to boost students' ability to sequence events.

1. Remind students that K.C. did a number of "unspeakable" things to Grady's bear. Ask students what these seven things were; write them on the board or overhead as children dictate. Then, assign each student an event to draw; be sure to assign each event to an equal number of students, if possible. After everyone has finished their picture, arrange students in small groups (7 students per group); each group should have pictures of all 7 things that K.C. did to the bear. Next, have each group sequence their pictures in the proper order. Children may simply lay their pictures in order on a table top or on the floor; for a neat variation, children can clothespin their pictures to a line hung across the classroom ceiling or tape them to a hallway wall.

2. For a more complicated variation of the first activity, substitute the sequence of events Grandpa followed to repair the bear for the sequence K.C. followed to destroy it.

Using Map and Globe Skills

Grady and Grandpa's bus trip introduces activities that build students' map and globe skills. For all of these activities, use the map shown at the end of the chapter.

1. For students without prior experiences with maps, use an overhead transparency of the sample map to introduce the "basics" of map use. Discuss maps with children; cover such points as the purpose of maps, the variety of maps, and a working definition of a map. Explain to children that maps are like pictures taken from overhead that we use to help locate places. Mark on the transparency one possible route that Grady and Grandpa might have taken to get downtown. Then, discuss alternate routes they might have followed with students; mark these other routes on the transparency as children dictate them.

2. If students have some knowledge of mapmaking, provide dittoes of the sample map for each student. Briefly review what maps are, how we use them, and why they are used. Working in pairs, students may make on their maps a possible route that Grady and Grandpa could have taken to get downtown. Have each pair use their map to explain their choice of routes to the class. To follow up this activity, students may compare their choices in terms of efficiency and ease of travel; the class may select a "quickest" or an "easiest" route for Grady and Grandpa.

Practicing Social Interaction

The story emphasizes several "cardinal principles" of social interaction that can be explored further in the following activities.

1. After reading the book aloud, go over the story's key events with students (K.C. arrives, becomes "difficult," Grady's parents ask him to share his bear, K.C. abuses the bear, etc.). Focus on Grady's sharing with K.C. Discuss this key event in the story using the following questions to generate student responses.

   a. Was it easy for Grady to share his bear? Why not?
   b. Why did Grady share his bear?
   c. Was sharing the right thing to do? Why? Why not?
   d. What are some things you have shared?
   e. Why did you share them?

2. Remind children that Grady's bear was very special to him. Ask children to name things that are special to them. Give children a "homework" assignment: bring something from home that is as important to them as Grady's bear was to him; if this special thing is fragile or hard to move, students may draw a picture or bring a photo of it. The following day, have children "share" these special possessions (or photos or pictures) in a "show-and-tell" session; have children describe their item and relate why it is so special. Tell students that what they have just done is a form of sharing.

Depending on the level of trust and maturity of your first graders, consider asking them to share their special things physically as well as verbally.

Be sure to discuss the responsibilities inherent in sharing (the sharer must allow his special thing to be used; the sharee must be sure to use it carefully) before items change hands. Be sure that participants in this physical sharing are *volunteers*. Remember that damage to a special item can be most traumatic!

GRADY'S NEIGHBORHOOD

GRADY'S
HOUSE ☒

BUS STOP
☒

DOWNTOWN

CHAPTER SEVEN
The Patchwork Quilt
by Valerie Flournoy

The recipient of numerous honors in 1985-86, including: the Coretta Scott King Award for Illustrations; selection as a "Children's Choices" book; and listing among the NCSS's "Notable Trade Books in the Social Studies," *Booklist* magazine's "Children's Editors' Choices," and the New York Public Library's "One Hundred Titles for Reading and Sharing." Also, the book was featured on PBS's "Reading Rainbow" series.

Spache Readability Level—4+
Fry Readability Level—4

Flournoy, Valerie. *The Patchwork Quilt*. Pictures by Jerry Pinkney. New York: Dial Books (E.P. Dutton), 1985. Unpaged (approx. 30 pages). ISBN 0-8037-0097-0 and 0-8037-0098-9 (library binding).

Flournoy's moving story recounts a family effort to "invest" memories in a patchwork quilt. As Tanya watches in fascination, Grandma begins cutting, patching, and sewing one spring afternoon. The elderly woman joins bits and pieces of brother Jim's favorite pants, Papa's workshirt, Mama's gold dress, Tanya's Halloween costume, and Ted's red shirt. Grandma tells Tanya that a "quilt won't forget," because each block stores part of the past. Grandma's sudden illness devastates the family, particularly Tanya, who fears that her grandmother's project will never be finished. Slowly, lovingly, the family unites to make Grandma's vision a reality. Tanya dedicates most afternoons to sewing the masterpiece. As the quilt becomes more complete, Grandma gains strength. She recovers in time to put finishing touches on her dream and present it to Tanya, who cherishes this storehouse of a family's love.

Relationship to Social Studies

Flournoy has written a tender story with several direct links to a dominant theme of first grade social studies teaching, "the family." Tanya's family, first of all, models many positive qualities (loyalty, love, etc.) lacked by many homes in today's fast-paced society. By setting her story in a Black household, the author also promotes multicultural awareness and undermines stereotypes some youngsters hold about minority families.

Additionally, Tanya's example might well enhance student's affective growth. Her determination and responsibility are traits that should be encouraged in all children. The book also suggests activities that build students' ability to perceive time relationships and communicate their feelings to others through visual media. Flournoy's work, moreover, introduces quilt-making projects that provide opportunities for students to work productively in small groups.

For its many strengths, *The Patchwork Quilt* contains complex vocabulary and concepts that might not be familiar for small children. As a result, the book is best read aloud. Teachers should also allow time to discuss words and ideas that children find confusing. And, as always, teachers need to substitute words or paraphrase paragraphs to increase flow and comprehension of the story.

Developing Communication Skills

The following activities use quilt-making to foster children's ability to communicate orally, nonverbally, and through visual imagery.

1. After reading the story aloud, discuss quilt-making with children. Convey the notion that quilts communicate a craftsperson's feelings and heritage as well as being works of art. Introduce common quilt patterns to children ("Bear's Paw," "Dresden Plate," etc.) and provide them with background information about the craft. Then, invite a quilt-maker to visit the class and display her work. Children should know enough about quilts to ask questions. Encourage the speaker to share the "messages" that she has tried to communicate through her quilts.

2. Read the story aloud, then discuss the many things that Tanya's new quilt communicated about her family. Introduce a major class project to students—they will each make a quilt square that holds personal message and then combine squares to communicate the class's story. If sewing cloth squares is beyond students' fine motor skills, use a simpler medium (colored paper or cloth scraps pasted to 6″×6″ blocks of construction paper). Individual quilt squares can be joined in several ways (sewn together, glued to sheets of butcher paper, etc.). Display the class quilt. Review its messages with students at a later date.

3. To follow-up the second activity, generate an oral history of hthe class quilt. Have each student dictate an explanation of his/her square into a tape recorder. Play the tape at a later date to help students understand the many messages in their class quilt. Use the tape to introduce the quilt to visitors (parents, administrators, other classes, etc.)

Nurturing the Affective Domain

The story suggests several sharing sessions in which children may relate Tanya's experiences to their own situations. After reading the book aloud, discuss the following passages with students.

1. Papa says that he "had never felt so much happiness in the house," after the family's Christmas celebration. Have children describe times when their houses were happy places. To extend this activity, children may write (or dictate to a "secretary" or to a tape recorder) two ways in which they might make their houses happier places.

2. Early in the story, Grandma tells Mama that a patchwork quilt is much more than "a quilt from any department store." Ask children what ingredients a patchwork quilt contains that sets it apart from a store-bought bedspread. To extend the discussion, ask children how those special ingredients get into a patchwork quilt.

Promoting Thinking Skills

After reading *The Patchwork Quilt* to students,

use the following activities to foster several important aspects of critical thinking.

1. Review the main events of Tanya's story with the class. Then, divide students into pairs; have each pair draw a key event from the story. To conclude this activity, the class constructs a "living" timeline with these drawings (i.e. the groups, displaying their pictures, arrange themselves in correct order along a classroom wall or corridor). As much as possible, allow the class to determine when the proper sequence has been achieved.

2. Remind students that Grandma and Mama "sign" the quilt before presenting it to Tanya. Ask children why they took the time to incribe their names on this masterpiece. Brainstorm a list of other things that must be signed before they are considered finished. Help students classify these items; guide them to some conclusions about the types of things that carry the signatures of their creators.

Using Map and Globe Skills

Follow a "read-aloud" session with this activity in which children discover as much as they can about the place where Tanya and her family live. Slowly reread the story with children; collect as much information about the story's setting as children can provide (data like, "Tanya's house has a backyard;" "her house has two stories;" "Tanya lives in a place where it is warm in the summer, but cold in the winter;" etc.). Gradually, help children form a "mental picture" of what Tanya's house looked like. Provide time for children to translate their images into drawings of Tanya's home. Allow students to share and discuss their pictures. Working with class input, construct a simple map of Tanya's residence on the chalkboard or overhead. Discuss the ways in which this map provides a better understanding of where Tanya lives than the "mental pictures" or drawings.

Practicing Social Interaction

A class quilt-making project offers children tremendous opportunities to practice a crucial aspect of social interaction—working cooperatively to attain a common goal. Your students' abilities will dictate the materials you use to create your class quilt; even with able students, consider an alternative to a hand-sewn product (such as cloth or paper scraps glued to heavy paper squares). Depending on the nature of your class, this project may be structured in a variety of ways, including:

1. Each child makes a quilt block; the whole class determines how the completed blocks will be arranged to complete the quilt.

2. Children work in small groups (2-3 students each) to complete quilt blocks; a student committee decides how the quilt is best assembled.

3. Each child makes a quilt block; small groups of students assemble individual blocks into quilt sections; the teacher, working from whole-class input, joins the sections to create the finished quilt.

The specific structure you select is not that important. The crucial thing is providing chances for your students to experience the group decision-making process.

CHAPTER EIGHT

Like Jake and Me
by Mavis Jukes

Chosen as a Newbery Honor book in 1985; included amoung "Notable Trade Books in the Social Studies" (1984) and "Children's Choices" (1985)

Spache Readability Level—4 +
Fry Readability Level—2

Juke, Mavis. **Like Jake and Me**. Pictures by Lloyd Bloom. New York: Alfred A. Knopf, 1984. Unpaged (approx. 32 pages). ISBN 0-394-85608-2 and 0-394-95608-7 (library binding).

With fast-paced dialogue and expressive, pastel illustrations, Jukes and Bloom chronicle a day in which three off-beat characters recognize their mutual love and become a family. Alex worships his new dad—a living, breathing cowboy named Jake, who seems larger, stronger, and braver than anyone the young boy can imagine. As hard as he tries, Alex cannot generate a friendship with Jake as loving and caring as his relationship with his mother, Virginia. Finally, a comical "emergency"—a wolf spider crawling into Jake's clothes—brings stepfather and son together. Alex learns that cowboys can be frightened by the littlest critters; Jakes sees that a small boy can be a resourceful rescuer. To celebrate their victory over the wolf spider, Alex and Jake whirl about the porch as if to show the world that they are father and son at last..

Relationship to Social Studies

First grade social studies programs commonly examine family life in some depth. *Like Jake and Me* shares this focus on family and can be an excellent resource for these programs as a result. The book offers young readers the example of people who grow together till they model the qualities that any positive family setting must demonstrate. Jukes, moreover, peoples her story with some genuine "characters" whose family situation can certainly be termed "non-traditional." Students need to see that a boy can find acceptance and love in his second family after his mother and natural father divorce. Children can learn a great deal of social studies by examining the alternative lifestyle and unique location which Alex's family experiences.

As with many picture books, the story explores concepts and uses vocabulary much more complex than one might expect from such a work. Jukes, moreover, presents persistently "different" characters who treat pregnancy, tattoos, and a brief glimpse of nudity in matter-of-fact fashion. Consequently, the book is best delivered in a "read-aloud" session with time for discussion of unfamiliar words beforehand and unfamiliar ideas afterward.

Developing Communication Skills

Jukes offers a humorous conversation between Jake and Alex midway through the story. This interchange introduces the following activities in which children examine miscommunication.

1. After reading the story to the class, reread the passage in which Alex talks about the female wolf spider and Jake is convinced that Alex is referring to his mother, Virginia. Analyze this interchange in depth with students. Help them find elements of the conversation that caused Alex and Jake to miscommunicate. Ask them how Jake and Alex could have avoided miscommunication. Conclude the activity by developing some "rules" that might help children communicate more clearly and effectively.

2. Try the activity above with an interesting variation—rather than rereading Jake and Alex's

talk, have two students role play it for the class. To extend this activity further, let children role play similar "misconversations" that might occur in their classroom before generating the "rules" of effective communication.

3. As a follow-up to the first activity, divide children into small groups (no more than 2-3 students per group) and have them role play situations where clear communication is necessary (i.e. telling a police officer about an accident; settling a dispute on the ball field; etc.). Remind them to follow the rules for effective communication developed earlier.

Nurturing the Affective Domain

The book suggests a range of activities in which children explore feelings they might share with Alex and Jake.

1. Read the story aloud, then discuss Jake's encounter with the wolf spider. Use the comical incident to help children deal with their own fears; guide them to the conclusion that all people are frightened to some degree; it is natural to be afraid. Consider the following questions to stimulate discussion:
   a. Was Jake afraid of the wolf spider? How can you tell?
   b. Did you expect that Jake would be frightened? Why? Why not?
   c. Would you have been afraid of the spider like Jake?
   d. Are there any other things that might make you afraid?
   e. How did Jake deal with his fears?
   f. How might you deal with the things that frighten you?

2. Read the story aloud, then talk about Jake and Alex's feelings toward one another. Ask children to support their responses with information from the story.

3. After reading the story to the class, discuss the nature of Jake and Alex's relationship (stepfather and stepson). Ask children:
   a. Imagine you are Alex. Is it difficult to have a father and a stepfather? Why? Why not?
   b. Imagine you are Jake. Would it be difficult to gain a stepson like Alex?

How might you feel toward your new stepson? What could you do to get along better with your new son?

Like Jake and Me introduces activities in which children hone their abilities to predict and to conceptualize. Read the book to your class, then use one or all of the following experiences.

1. Examine the nature of Alex's family with children; label the type of family in which Alex lives (a "step-parent family"). Next, talk about other types of families, label them, and list these terms on the chalkboard or overhead. Discuss the ways in which these many types of families are different (number of members, relationships of members, etc.). More importantly, discuss the many features that these types of families have in common. To conclude the activity, generate a list of characteristics that all families share.

2. Remind children of the fact that Virginia is about to have twins. Discuss this situation with children. Ask any twins or siblings of twins in your class to share their experiences. Use the following questions to help students speculate about the impact of these twins on Alex's family.

    a. Will the twins be boys or girls or both?

    b. How soon will the twins arrive?

    c. How will the twins act? What will they do?

    d. How will the twins change Alex's life? Jake's? Virginia's?

    e. Will Alex's family be changed in any way? How?

To extend this activity, children may draw a "photograph" of the twins or a portrait of Alex's family after their arrival.

3. Reread the last pages of the story and discuss the change in Alex and Jake's relationship that this ending suggests. Speculate with children about how Alex and Jake might interact in the future. Divide students into small groups (3 per group); have each group create a day in the life of Alex and Jake six months after this story ended. Provide time for each group to share its efforts with the class.

Using Map and Globe Skills

The story's unspecified setting suggests activities which combine students' geographic and problem solving skills.

1. Read the story to children. Review clues to where the story occurs; focus students' attention on the vegetation that the author describes (pear and cypress trees). Assign "homework"—with their parents' assistance, students should research areas in our country in which this combination of trees might grow (the list will be fairly small). The next day, discuss these locations and show them on a United States map. Finally, decide, as a class, where *Like Jake and Me* probably took place.

2. To follow up the first activity, have students imagine that they are authors writing a story about a day with their father/guardian. They want to set the story in their hometown and to leave clues so that the reader can determine the approximate location in which the story happened. Brainstorm a list of geographic/cultural/natural features that the children might include in their story.

Practicing Social Interaction

This activity resembles one included in the section on promoting thinking skills. Begin by discussing the many different types of families and listing them on the chalkboard or overhead. Then, divide children into small groups; let the membership of each small group reflect a type of family that the class has listed (the "single-parent" group should have 2 members; the "mother-father-child" group should have 3 members; etc.). Have the groups talk about ways in which they might get along better as a family and share their findings with the class. To extend the activity, provide the groups with a scenario (for example: "Your family needs to decide where you will take your vacation."); have them role play this situation to implement the guidelines for better family relations that they have previously discussed.

CHAPTER NINE

I Go with My Family to Grandma's
by Riki Levinson

Listed among 1986's "Notable Trade Books in the Social Studies."

Spache Readability Level—4 +
Fry Readability Level—5

Levinson, Riki. *I Go with My Family to Grandma's*. Illustrated by Diane Goode. New York: E.P. Dutton, 1986. Unpaged (approx. 32 pages). ISBN 0-525-44261-8.

With strong support from Goode's naturalistic drawings, Levinson needs just 122 words to capture the exhuberance, warmth, and joy of a very special family's reunion. Five cousins and their families, living in turn-of-the-century New York City, journey to Grandma's eastside brownstone for a special family dinner. Each family lives in a different borough of the city and uses different modes of transportation to reach Grandma's. When everyone arrives, thirty-six relatives jam Grandma's house and share the special joy that being together as a family brings.

Relationship to Social Studies

Levinson's story allows the creative social studies teacher to acquaint first graders with aspects of "family" that they might not otherwise encounter. The book, first of all, describes a family much larger and more complex than those that children typically encounter today. This family, moreover, lives in a time (the early twentieth century) and a setting (a teeming, bustling city) that most children will find unfamiliar. Also, family members travel in ways alien to many youngsters.

These "different" elements of the story, moreover, suggest activities that build important social studies skills. In the area of critical thinking, for example, children may compare and contrast their own daily life with a quite different situation. The travels of the story's characters provide content for simple map exercises.

For all its value as a social studies resource, the book is not as readable as it might first appear. The brief plot and simple sentence structure mask some advanced vocabulary and complex ideas. Consequently, the book is best read aloud to a large group of students. Once exposed to the story, students can enjoy the straightforward prose and colorful illustrations individually or in small groups.

Developing Communication Skill

I Go with My Family to Grandma's offers children chances to practice both visual and written forms of communication.

1. After reading the story aloud, point out a dilemma to the group—Grandma did not have a phone; how did she invite all her family for dinner? After the group considers this issue, brainstorm ways in which Grandma might have communicated her invitation to the five branches of her family.

2. To follow up the previous activity, tell children that Grandma has asked their help. She wants each of them to write a letter to either Millie, Bella, Carrie, Beatie, or Stella inviting her and her family to Sunday dinner; letters should be signed, "Love, Grandma." Students without the necessary writing skills may dictate their letters to an adult

or older student volunteer. Children may share their letters if time permits.

3. Read the book to students; discuss the ways in which the author communicated her story to her readers. Guide children to the observation that the illustrations were at least as important a means of communicating the story as the printed word. Examine selected drawings with students and discuss the many things that each picture communicates about Grandma's family.

To extend this activity, take polaroid photos of your classroom over the course of a day; discuss with students what these photos communicate about your class. Conclude with the observation that, in some cases, "a picture *is* worth a thousand words!"

Nurturing the Affective Domain

Within this seemingly simple story, the author has imbedded deep, intimate feelings. The book affords children chances to explore similar emotions that they might have through the following activities.

1. Examine one (or more) of the family pictures near the end of the book. Speculate with children about the feelings that each person in the illustration(s) might have. If time permits, volunteers can share times when they had similar feelings. To extend this activity further, children can draw a portrait of their own families.

2. Show children the pictures in which Grandma and Grandpa greet family members as they arrive. Let children look at these illustrations carefully. Discuss the emotions that each person in the pictures must feel. Let volunteers tell about occasions when they also had these feelings. To extend the activity, children may draw a picture of a time when they greeted new arrivals at their house or role play one of the greeting sessions pictured in the book.

Promoting Thinking Skills

I Go with My Family to Grandma's provides content for experiences that encourage students' classification and comparison skills. Read the story to students, then introduce the following activities.

1. Have students list the modes of transportation that the five cousins used to reach Grandma's. Create simple categories (i.e. "vehicles that hold many people" and "vehicles that hold a few people") in which children classify these modes of transportation. Then, devise new categories (i.e. "vehicles that use muscle power," "animal powered vehicles," and "machine powered vehicles") and have students re-classify. Repeat this process several times.

2. Select one of the story's more vivid two-paged illustrations. Over the course of a day, make the book available for students to examine this picture individually or in small groups. The next day, analyze this picture as a class. Look at aspects of daily life shown in the picture (such as, clothing, housing, transportation, furniture, hairstyles, etc.). For each of these categories, have students compare and contrast what is shown in the picture with the way things are today. Finally, show children various media (slides, photos, etc.) that capture daily life in times past and today; ask children to determine whether each picture happened "now" or "a long time ago" and have them defend their responses.

Using Map and Globe Skills

Read the book aloud and review the basic story line with children. Then, display a simple map of New York City and introduce the following activities that build students' geographic skills.

1. Using colored or "flagged" pins, help student volunteers mark the approximate location of the homes of each family group in the story. Follow clues left by the author to find and mark Grand-

ma's house (on the east side of Manhattan, under the Brooklyn Bridge).

2. Trace the route that each family group might have traveled to Grandma's. Mark these routes on the map.

3. Compare the routes that each family group took to Grandma's. Ask children:

    a. Which family **took** the shortest journey? the longest?

    b. Whose trip was the most difficult? Why?

Practicing Social Interaction:

Read and discuss the story with children. Leave children with the observation that this story occurred a long time ago, when life was somewhat different than it is now. As in a previous activity, make the book available over the course of a day for children to examine in small groups. Before they look at the book, tell students that they are detectives hunting for ways that children used to have fun 75 years ago.

The next day, meet in a large group session and discuss the toys and games that the class discovered in the book's pictures. Focus on the games that children played and list them on the chalkboard; the list should include: ball & cup, stick & hoop, ball-toss games, cards, jump rope, and tag. Review rules for these games with children.

Then, take children to the playground. Divide them into small groups and let them play as many of these "ancient" games as time permits. After children have returned inside, discuss their experiences with these games. Ask children if the games were fun; if they resembled any games children have already played; and, if they would like to play them again.

CHAPTER TEN

The Relatives Came
by Cynthia Rylant

A Caldecott Honor book, 1986; also included among
"Notable Trade Books in the Social Studies" that same year.

Spache Readability Level—4 +
Fry Readability Level—7

Rylant, Cynthia. **The Relatives Came**. Illustrated by Stephen Gammell. New York: Bradbury Press, 1985.
Unpaged (approx. 28 pages). ISBN 0-02-777220-9.

In this wildly humorous tale, Rylant shares reminiscences of a summer past when kinfolk visited, stayed
for what seemed like months, and made home a much more joyous place to be. The relatives "came up
from Virignia" in a battle-scarred station wagon, driving all day and half the night. They swept into the
yard and the hugging began almost before their car had stopped. Too much hugging, lots of talking, some
heavy-duty overeating, and plenty of laughter accompanied the relatives for the weeks and weeks and weeks
that they stayed. Finally, but still all-too-soon, the relatives headed back to Virginia, leaving lots of happy
memories and a house that was much too quiet.

Relationship to
Social Studies

The book's language, involved sentence structure, and subtle humor make it difficult reading for young children. Rylant writes with a sophistication that makes her work seem almost more adult than early childhood fare. Reading this book aloud seems the only viable way to deliver its content to students. Pre- and post-reading discussion also seem mandatory.

While not an easy book, *The Relatives Came* can contribute so much to a primary level social studies program that any struggle to understand confusing passages is well-worth a child's effort. Rylant, first of all, captures the excitement, love, silliness, fun, chaos, and affection that any family gathering generates. She vividly portrays the emotional dimension of family life for young readers. The author also offers a "different" family model that children should encounter—a large, rural family gathering set in the not-so-distant past.

Rylant's work, moreover, suggests social studies skill-building activities in a number of key areas— including communication, maps and globes, social interaction, and critical thinking. For first grade social studies programs concerned with "family," the book can yield many benefits.

Developing
Communication Skills

The Relatives Came can introduce any number of activities that encourage students' abilities to communicate orally and in writing. Several possibilities are listed below.

1. Read the story to children and discuss why the relatives appeared one summer evening. Did they just decide to come? Probably not. Were they invited? Seems likely. Proceed from this premise and consider the most effective media for this invitation (phone? letter?). Then pair children and have them take turns role-playing a phone conversation in which they invite favorite relatives to visit during an upcoming vacation. To extend this activity, have children dictate a letter inviting these relatives to visit. Take time to share these experiences with the class.

2. Read the story to children and explain to them that it is an example of an oral history—a personal account of an event that someone remembered and recorded so that others can appreciate the experience. Have children reflect on an important event in their lives (a trip or a visit from relatives or the arrival of a new sister) then tape record their rememberances of this experience. If time allows, listen to these "oral histories" as a class.

3. Have the children draw a picture of 2-4 relatives outside of their homes who come to visit occasionally. Print their names below the pictures.

Nurturing the
Affective Domain

The book suggests activities in which children consider feelings of sadness and attitudes about the "strange and different."

1. Read the book aloud and establish a chronology of events with students. Focus discussion on the relatives' journey, with emphasis on a passage early in the story, "While they traveled along, they looked at the *strange* houses and *different* mountains..."

Ask children to share things they have seen that seemed "strange and different." Were there things and places in their own lives that were once strange, perhaps even scary, but which they now like. For example, was their school building strange and scary the first time they saw it? How about now? Discuss why things might seem "strange and different" to us, but perfectly average to other people. Guide students to the conclusion that "strange and different" does not necessarily mean "bad and wrong."

2. Read the story to children, then discuss the ending. Ask children:
    a. Is it a happy ending? a sad ending? Why?
    b. Why does the family feel this way after their relatives leave?
    c. Why do the relatives feel as they do?
    d. How would you feel if you were the family? the relatives?

To conclude the activity, have children share their feelings after leaving a family gathering and compare them with the feelings of characters in the story.

3. Have children make a "different" kind of

animal out of modelling clay. Allow time for the children to play with their animals.

Assign them the task of telling others in class why he/she loves this animal. When other children remark negatively about the looks of an animal, have its creator stick up for it by stating that the animal may look different "but that's only because you don't know it as well as I do!"

Promoting Thinking Skills

The great quantities of food consumed in the story provide content for a variety of classification and decision-making activities. First, read the story aloud. Next, generate a list of all the foods pictured or mentioned in the story. Then, try one (or all) of the following activities.

1. Children find pictures of these foods in magazines and newspapers, working either individually, in pairs, or in small groups.

2. Children discuss their experiences with these foods (to guide this discussion you might ask, "Which have you eaten?", "When?", "Which do you like?", "Which to you dislike?", "Why?").

3. Children classify these foods into the major food groups. You may simply list food names under categories written on the chalkboard; for an interesting twist, have children fasten the pictures they found in the first activity to sheets of butcher paper with category labels.

4. To reinforce understanding of good nutrition, have children plan healthy meals using the foods found in Rylant's story.

Using Map and Globe Skills

Build children's awareness of spatial relationships and location with the following activities introduced by the story.

1. Read the story aloud and focus discussion on the relatives' journey, particularly on the recurring phrase, "and up they came—from Virginia." Locate Virginia on a large, simple map of the United States. Review the length of the relatives' trip ("they drove all day long and into the night").

Considering the era in which they traveled (1950's) and the mountainous terrain, assume the trip was about 300 miles. With the map scale as a reference, cut a string to indicate that distance. Then, using the string as a guide, speculate with children where the story took place (remember, the relatives traveled "up" or north from Virginia). Review helpful "clues" the author provides to narrow the possible locations (the story's setting is a rural area, mountainous, etc.). Let class consensus determine the most likely area where Rylant's tale took place.

2. Prior to your next class field trip involving bus travel, reread the story with students and review passages in which the narrator describes things that the relatives saw on their trip. Divide students into small groups that will sit together on the bus. Give groups the task of observing and remembering features encountered on the trip (unusual buildings, landforms, rivers and lakes, vegetation, etc.). On the day after the field trip, take time to review these observations as a large group.

Practicing Social Interaction

In addition to the small group lessons already proposed, the book introduces a role play activity which reinforces children's ability to interact productively in a large group situation.

Begin by reading the story aloud and examining the pictures of its many colorful characters. Allow the class to brainstorm names for each of these people. Make nametags for enough characters to provide an identity for all of your students (you may have to create a few additional identities depending on class enrollment).

Once nametags and other preparations are completed, have a "family reunion" in your classroom. Review the notion of assuming different identities, reexamine the pictures of each character to firm identities in children's minds, and discuss appropriate behavior at a large gathering. When the "reunion" has run its course, conclude with a discussion of what children learned from this experience.

CHAPTER ELEVEN

Jim's Dog Muffins
by Miriam Cohen

Cited among "Notable Trade Books in the Social Studies," 1984.

Spache Readability Level—4+
Fry Readability Level—2

Cohen, Miriam. ***Jim's Dog Muffins***. Pictures by Lilian Hoban. New York: Greenwillow Books, 1984. Unpaged (approx. 28 pages). ISBN 0-688-02564-1.

In a sensitive and true-to-life fashion, Cohen and Hoban describe a boy's reaction to the heartbreaking
death of his dog. When a truck runs over Muffins, Jim can hardly contain his sadness. His first grade classmates try everything to ease his loss—they write him a letter, tell him they are sorry, and try to cheer him
up. But nothing works, and Jim just mopes and daydreams all day. On the way home, Paul buys himself
and Jim slices of pizza, and eats his in the silly way the boys always enjoyed pizza. Jim laughs, then cries,
then tells his friend how much he misses Muffins. Paul agrees that Muffins was a good dog. As the boys
walk, Jim feels a little better now that he knows a friend understands.

Relationship to Social Studies

Cohen and Hoban team to create a work with great potential as a resource for second grade social studies. First, they accurately depict classroom routine in a neighborhood elementary school. A multi-ethnic group of children populate this classroom and interact in the humorously direct ways that "real-life" youngsters would. This model provides content for lessons that boost multicultural awareness and social interaction skills.

Additionally, the book has an affective dimension that can contribute strongly to social studies teaching. A deep personal loss confronts Jim — a loss that young children can easily understand. Jim's reaction to his tragedy, his friends' sometimes misguided sympathy, and the manner in which Jim copes with his dog's death are examples that might profit children facing a similar heartbreak.

Jim's Dog Muffins can be read aloud to large or small groups of students. At the same time, the story is not beyond the reading abilities of many second grade readers. Students, either individually or in teams, may read the story if an appropriate situation arises.

Developing Communication Skills

Events in Cohen's book introduce the practice of expressing sympathy to someone who has lost a loved one. Read the story to a group of students and then consider the following activities in which children communicate sympathy orally and in writing.

1. Review the passage in which Jim's classmates "wrote" him a letter expressing sympathy after Muffins' death. Discuss with students why people write sympathy letters and the form they typically take. Then, help students identify someone in their class, other classes, or the school staff who has recently experienced a loss as painful as Jim's. Depending on their language proficiency, have students write individual sympathy letters to this person or dictate a group letter to you or an aide. Once the letter(s) are polished into final form, appoint a committee to deliver the letter(s) on behalf of the class.

2. Reread portions of the story in which Jim's classmates try to console him. Discuss what one might say in such situations. Let children role play brief scenarios in which they comfort a friend who has suffered a loss like Jim's. Conclude the activity by reviewing what is helpful to say at these times and what is not so helpful.

Nurturing the Affective Domain

The book suggests activities that foster two crucial aspects of students' affective growth — becoming multiculturally aware and dealing with grief.

1. Read the story to students and discuss the range of behaviors that characters demonstrated (Danny's bluntness, Paul's concern, Jim's anger, etc.). Help children classify these behaviors into two categories: "actions that hurt" and "actions that helped." Review specific instances in which behaviors from the first category hurt characters in the story; talk about actions from the second category that seemed to help. Discuss why these actions hurt or helped. To extend the activity, provide the class with scenarios involving people experiencing grief. Ask volunteers what actions they would take to help these situations.

2. Read the book aloud, then establish a chronology of Jim's actions. Discuss the motivation for these actions with students; help them understand the deep emotions that made Jim behave as he did. Let volunteers share times in which they acted as Jim did and the emotions that prompted them to act this way.

3. After reading the story aloud, discuss Jim's class. Begin by describing the group statistically (total number of students, of girls, of boys, etc.). Shift the discussion to the differences among class members, specifically racial/cultural characteristics that separated them. Move to a comparison of the many similarities these children shared.

Then, have children contrast the differences and compare the similarities in their own class. To end the activity, guide students to the observation that any group has differences, but also similarities that bind its members together.

Promoting Thinking Skills

For all activities that build students' ability to think critically, begin by reading the book aloud, then list the behaviors that Jim demonstrated over the course of the story (i.e. missed school, refused to talk, wouldn't listen, etc.). Armed with this list of Jim's actions, students are ready for the following learning experiences.

1. Assign pairs of students the task of drawing one of Jim's actions from the list generated earlier. Have the class sequence these pictures in chronological order. Then, help students determine cause-effect relationships that exist between these events (i.e. Muffins' death and Jim's missing school; Jim's yelling at Anna Marie and his separation from his classmates; Jim's crying and his feeling better).

2. Examine Jim's behaviors in totality; guide children to the conclusion that a grieving *process* exists and that people must experience all of it before they feel better. Discuss the crucial role of emotional release in this process; point out to students how Jim did not improve his attitude until he finally cried. Ask children if the grieving process varies from person to person. Allow volunteers to share a time when they had such an experience.

Using Map and Globe Skills

Read the story aloud, then remind students that Jim did not choose a book for silent reading. Discuss why Jim refused to make a selection. Ask children if there are other reasons why students lack materials for silent reading sessions. Guide them to the observation that some children cannot find what they want to read in the library.

Then, briefly discuss map-making with the class. Point out that people make maps of almost any place; they make maps to find specific locations and things. Tell students that we often map libraries to help people discover needed materials.

Arrange for your class to work with the school librarian (or library aide) on a "mapping the library" project. Provide students with outline maps of the library's major features. With the librarian's assistance, have students identify important parts of their school library and mark them on their map outlines. Briefly discuss what students learned about their library to conclude the activity.

Practicing Social Interaction

The story's characters model several situations that are obvious possibilities for promoting your students' interaction skills. Read the story to children, then consider implementing the following activities.

1. Reread the passage describing the cooking lesson in which Jim's class made vegetable soup. Have your class make soup; send a delegation to invite the principal, and enjoy a soup lunch with your guest of honor. To add spice to this activity, consider the following variations: hold a class referendum to determine the type of soup you will make; divide the class into small groups (each under adult supervision) and allow each group to make a different type of soup; invite parents or other visitors to join the principal as luncheon guests of honor.

2. Implement regular SSR ("Sustained Silent Reading") in your classroom. Follow the example of Jim's teacher and let children read any materials they wish silently every day at a certain time. To extend the activity, send delegations to other primary classrooms to encourage their participation in your SSR project. Try to involve the entire school (includig cooks, janitors, principal, and secretaries!) in SSR.

CHAPTER TWELVE

The Crack-of-Dawn Walkers
by Amy Hest

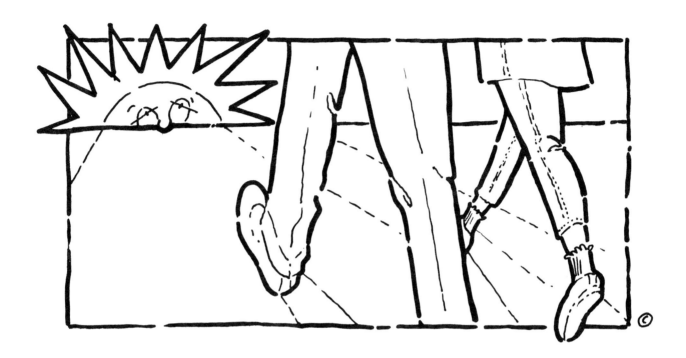

An IRA/CBC "Children's Choices" selection for 1985.

Spache Readability Level—4 +
Fry Readability Level—4

Hest, Amy. **The Crack-of-Dawn Walkers**. Pictures by Amy Schwartz. New York: Macmillan, 1984. Unpaged (approx. 32 pages). ISBN 0-02-743710-8.

Hest drew upon recollections of rivalry with her own brother to write this story of children's possessiveness about special moments with a favorite relative. Sadie and Ben made a pact—they would no longer split time with Grandfather, but would take their early-morning walks with him separately, on alternate Sundays. On this particular Sunday, Sadie glories in the stops that she and Grandfther always make—at Emma's bakery for breakfast rolls and Fabio's candy store for coffee, cocoa, and a newspaper. On the walk home, Sadie acknowledges to Grandfather that she does love her brother, but not enough to share her special Sunday walks with him ever!.

Relationship to Social Studies

Hest and Schwartz's work relates to second grade social studies teaching in several ways. First of all, the book can broaden young children's understanding of the concept of "neighborhood." The area in which Sadie and Grandfather walk is a neighborhood in the traditional sense — family dwellings surrounding a business district of small shops where people live their entire lives and develop a strong sense of belonging. Children may compare and contrast this setting with a modern neighborhood — a place probably less congenial and more unstable than the area that the story's characters enjoy so much.

Secondly, the story offers content for lessons that build a number of social studies competencies — particularly map and globe skills. Finally, Sadie's jealousy of Ben and her possessiveness of Grandfather are common emotions for children; Sadie's example introduces experiences in which children confront similar attitudes and feelings.

The Crack-of-Dawn Walkers is not the best picture book for reading individually by young readers. The book, however, should hold students' interest well as a read-aloud selection, as long as time is taken for introductory and comprehension sessions before and after reading.

Developing Communication Skills

Hest's story introduces activities that encourage students' oral and written communication skills.

1. After listening to the story and discussing its plot, children may reflect on a special person with whom they might like to take a "crack-of-dawn" walk around their neighborhood. Children can also visualize a route for this neighborhood tour and several places they might visit along the way.

Have children write a letter to this special person inviting him/her on this walk; the letter should include the proposed itinerary. If possible, use the "process writing" approach to finalize these letters (i.e. each child drafts a letter, shares this first effort with a small group of classmates, rewrites the letter, submits it to the teacher for editing, then puts the letter into final form). If time permits, let volunteers share their letters with the class. Above all, encourage children to "follow-through" and deliver their invitations to their special people.

2. Read the story aloud, then focus discussion on the "peace treaty" between Sadie and Ben regarding their time spent with Grandfather. Review the terms of this agreement with children. Then, pair children and let them role play and negotiate the following scenario.

Each of the children in the pair decides upon a favorite adult with whom they would like to take a special walk. Child A tells about this person in some detail, especially why he/she is so nice. Child A then reports that this adult has also invited Child B along on the next walk with them. Now child A admits that he/she really would like to go alone with this adult. Child A then suggests negotiating. Let the talks begin!

The cards are reversed. Child B tells of his/her favorite adult, etc.

Nurturing the Affective Domain

Children may explore the Sadie-Ben relationship and draw parallels with their own situations in the following activities.

1. Read the story aloud, then help students generate a list of comments that Sadie made about her brother, Ben (i.e. "I'm glad Ben isn't here," "He talks too much," etc.). Then, analyze the nature of Sadie and Ben's relationship, using the following questions to prompt discussion.
   a. Do Sadie and Ben get along? Why do you think this way?
   b. Do Sadie and Ben really love each other? How can you tell?
   c. If they love each other, why won't they share Grandfather?

2. After completing the first activity, have children draw Sadie and Ben. To add a higher-level thinking element to students' drawings, have them portray Sadie and Ben together, interacting in a manner characteristic of their relationship. Provide time for children to explain their pictures.

3. After reading and discussing the story, have small groups of children (3 is most workable) write brief plays depicting a "day in the life" of Sadie and Ben. Instruct children to emphasize interac-

tions between brother and sister in their dramas. Once groups complete their plays, they may dramatize their efforts for the entire class. Assist children by having each group use the following positions: "Sadie," "Ben," and "Narrator" or "Sounds Director."

Promoting Thinking Skills

Grandfather's references to the "old country" suggest several activities that raise students' thinking to a higher level and also integrate geographic skill-building with this critical thinking. Read the story aloud, then discuss Grandfather's comments involving the "old country." Ask children why Grandfather mentioned this place; guide children to the observation that Grandfather was an immigrant (be sure children understand this term) and called his former home the "old country." From this introduction, move to one or all of the following activities.

1. On a world map, let children play detectives and discover the location of Grandfather's "old country." Reread the story for "clues."

2. Assign "homework:" have children ask their parents about the "old country" that their ancestors left to come to America. The following day, use colored or flagged pins to plot these locations on a world map. To conclude this activity, see if children can make any generalizations about immigration patterns from this map.

3. Discuss the reasons why people left their "old countries" to come to America. Ask children if all immigrants wanted to leave their former homes to live in this country. Generate a list of reasons why a person might have left the "old country." To follow-up this activity, have children research the reasons their ancestors left their "old country" and report back to the class.

Using Map and Globe Skills

Read the book to children, then introduce the following activities to build children's map-making skills.

1. Children draw a simple map of Sadie's neighborhood, showing the route that she and Grandfather took on Sunday mornings.

2. Children construct a map of the neighborhood in which your school is located. To liven this activity, make this a 3-dimensional map complete with model houses, plastic cars, and paper trees.

3. This activity continues the first lesson described in the section, "Developing Communication Skills." After children plan their "crack-of-dawn" walk with their special person, have them sketch a simple map of the route they will follow through the neighborhood. Children may present these maps to their guest as they begin their special walk.

Practicing Social Interaction

Read the story to children and discuss its main events briefly. Then, begin planning a class walk similar to the walk that Sadie and Grandfather enjoyed so much. Appoint committees to determine choice spots to stop along the way, map the proposed route, draft a permission letter to parents, and assemble any "supplies" the class might need. In a class meeting, brainstorm catchy names for your group of hikers ("the After-Lunch Bunch," perhaps?) and then select a nickname for the class by consensus.

Review the proposed route and itinerary as a large group and be sure they meet with class approval. Take your hike and discuss what students learned from this experience the following day; in this concluding session, pay particular attention to uncovering things students learned about working together to complete a class project.

To extend this activity, consider the following:

1. After the walk is completed, have students draw maps of the route they traveled.

2. Ask small groups of students to draft letters inviting parent, school, and neighborhood "dignitaries" to walk along with the class.

3. Ask how many people they greeted on their walk. Talk about the importance of being friendly in a neighborhood. Ask if there is a difference between greeting people in the neighborhood they live in as opposed to the city at large. (This may differ according to local custom and parents' wishes.)

CHAPTER THIRTEEN

It's Mine!
by Leo Lionni

Chosen as a "Notable Trade Book in the Social Studies" in 1986.

Spache Readability Level—4 +
Fry Readability Level—3

Lionni, Leo. **It's Mine!**. New York: Alfred A. Knopf, 1986. Unpaged (approx. 32 pages). ISBN 0-394-87000-4 (library binding).

Lionni crafts an upbeat fantasy in which characters learn the value of mutual understanding, cooperation, and a sense of common good. Three frogs inhabit an island in the middle of Rainbow Pond. Despite the beauty of their "neighborhood," Milton, Rupert, and Lydia cannot get along. Their bickering grows so intense that a neighbor, a giant toad, complains that he has no peace. Then one day, a ferocious thunderstorm strikes. Winds and rising water threaten the frogs' island. Their only chance of survival is to share a small rock until the flood subsides. The frogs follow the toad's advice and live together cooperatively. Their cry, "It's Mine!" becomes the motto, "It's Ours!"

Relationship to Social Studies

Part of the value of Lionni's work lies in its attractiveness—a captivating text reinforced by colorful, collage prints. The book's ability to hold children's interest should outweigh its somewhat difficult readability. The story's appeal should also heighten the impact of its many contributions to social studies teaching.

Lionni transports second grade readers to a mythical "neighborhood." Although a work of the author's imagination, this "neighborhood" offers children important lessons about conflict resolution, living in groups, and the negative aspects of possessive behavior. Lionni's story, moreover, presents children with an example of affective growth that they might emulate. The frogs' abandonment of selfishness and striving in favor of togetherness and cooperation is a transformation that children living in our sometimes too-competitive society should encounter. Finally, *It's Mine!* affords opportunities for students to practice a number of social studies-related skills, particularly map and globe, social interaction, and thinking skills.

Developing Communication Skills

Read *It's Mine!* to the class. After reviewing the plot, focus discussion on passages in which the frogs cannot get along. Ask children to describe how the frogs communicated with each other. (i.e. by quarreling, bickering, yelling, arguing, shouting, etc.). Ask children how these sessions made the frogs feel. Discuss whether or not this bickering accomplished anything. Then, implement one of the following activities that increase students' awareness of effective communication techniques.

1. Have students role play a "bicker session" (use an example from the book or develop your own scenario from an incident at school). Discuss the role play using the following questions to guide discussion:

   a. How would you describe the classroom during our "bicker session?"

   b. Did the session make the "bickerers" happy? Sad? Angry?

   c. What did the bickering accomplish? Anything?

   d. Is bickering a good way to communicate ideas? Why? Why not?

2. After establishing with students that the frogs argued all the time, ask them to consider whether arguing is always bad. Brainstorm situtations in which arguing allows people to communicate, even resolve differing viewpoints. Guide children to the observation that arguments must be controlled by rules to produce constructive outcomes.

Working individually, have students write 2-3 rules that might productively limit an argument. Then, divide students into small groups (3-4 students per group); let children share their rules with their small group; have each small group select three rules that they think are particularly helpful. To conclude the activity, ask a member to share each group's three selections. Edit these rules to create class guidelines that transform arguing into effective communication of differing viewpoints.

Nurturing the Affective Domain

The following activities encourage students' appreciation of individual differences and ability to resolve conflicts productively.

1. Read the book aloud, then talk about the toad's attempts to end the frogs' on-going conflict. Have students describe the toad's initial peacemaking effort (he asked the frogs to stop arguing) and his second intervention (rescuing the frogs from the flood in a way that encouraged their togetherness). Speculate with children why this later effort was more successful than the first.

Divide students into small groups (4 students each) and have the groups brainstorm other ways in which the toad might have stopped the frogs' "warfare." To culminate the activity, let each group present its alternative solutions that the toad might have tried. Extend this activity by having volunteers role play several of these alternatives.

2. After reading the story to children, point out that the toad helped his neighbors solve a nagging problem. Mention also that frogs and toads are quite different creatures even though they share some similarities. Discuss the differences between frogs and toads with students. Lead the class to the observation that people also have differences

that separate them and similarities that bind them together.

Briefly list some human differences. Help children understand that, like the toad and frogs, people frequently overcome these differences to solve mutual problems. Have students cut pictures of different sorts of people from newspapers and magazines. Then, have students use these photos to make collage-pictures that show different types of people uniting to solve a common problem. (Examples of problems might be pollution, war, hunger, dirty neighborhood streets, no jobs., etc.).

Promoting Thinking Skills:

It's Mine! suggests several activities that allow children to make decisions and critically analyze courses of action. Introduce these lessons by reading the book aloud and discussing its major events.

1. Review the situation that the toad faced early in the story (disruptive neighbors who argued loudly and constantly). Relate this situation to a similar problem the children might face at school or in their neighborhood (i.e. nearby students disrupting silent reading in the library; children fighting in a neighborhood yard; etc.). Next, introduce children to a systematic, orderly process for problem-solving; the handout shown at the end of this chapter outlines one possible decision-making model for children. Explain this process to children until they thoroughly understand it. Then, have children, working individually or in small groups, use this model to develop a response to the problem presented earlier. To conclude the activity, let volunteers share their solutions with the class.

2. Discuss the title Lionni chose for his book. Reread passages in which the frogs shout, "It's Mine!" Examine the logic of the frogs' claim with children (i.e. can someone own the air? the earth? the water?). Discuss why the frogs might have made such outrageous claims. Then, develop two lists on the chalkboard or overhead: things that people really might own and things that no one can ever really own. Compare/contrast these two lists; then, help children generate attributes that items on each list share so that they might better grasp the concept of "ownership."

Using Map and Globe Skills

Read the story to children, then focus their attention on Lionni's distinctive illustrations. Let children consider how the author created these pictures; analyze several pictures in terms of the materials and procedures Lionni used to construct them. Once children grasp the collage process, shift the discussion to the story's setting, Rainbow Pond. Establish the pond's major features and their relationship to each other. Then have children construct a "birds-eye" view of the pond using Lionni's artistic style (pieces of tissue, scraps of wrapping paper, and paper silhouettes glued on construction paper). Conclude the lesson with a sharing time and a brief discussion of how the "maps" the children made will help them better appreciate the story's setting.

Practicing Social Interaction

After reading the story aloud, discuss the nonproductive ways in which the frogs interacted. Then, divide children into small groups (about 5-6 students per group). Separate the groups as much as possible to prevent them from interrupting each other. Assign the groups a simple task: each member will share a happening in his/her neighborhood that they found interesting. Bring the class back together and discuss this experience. List factors that made the task go more smoothly for each group (i.e. waiting your turn to talk; not speaking loudly; not interrupting; etc.) talking out of turn; etc.). Conclude by establishing some class guidelines for more effective small group interaction.

MAKING DECISIONS

THE PROBLEM

CHOICE 1
GOOD
BAD

CHOICE 2
GOOD
BAD

CHOICE 3
GOOD
BAD

CHOICE 4
GOOD
BAD

CONSEQUENCES

MY DECISION

CHAPTER FOURTEEN

Music, Music for Everyone

by Vera B. Williams

One of the NCSS's "Notable Trade Books in the Social Studies" for 1984.

Spache Readability Level—4+
Fry Readability Level—2

Williams, Vera B. *Music, Music for Everyone*. New York: Greenwillow Books, 1984. Unpaged (approx. 32 pages). ISBN 0-688-02603-6 and 0-688-02604-4 (library binding).

Williams' words and pictures tell the story of a girl who learns a valuable lesson—hard work and dedication *do* pay-off. Rosa worried because the family money jar was almost empty. Grandma was ill and Mama worked as hard as she could. Rosa wished she could help in some way. One day, Rosa remembered that her other grandmother once earned money playing in a band. She recruited three musical friends, Jenny, Leora, and Mae, and formed the Oak Street Band. After practicing and practicing, the friends landed their first "gig" at a party celebrating the anniversary of Leora's great-grandparents. The band achieved critical acclaim as party guests danced into the night. Rosa's best feelings came later, though. As she deposited her share of the band's fee into the family money jar, Rosa knew that her hours of practicing had been worth it.

Relationship to Social Studies

Williams weaves joyful words and watercolors into a tale that delivers important citizenship models to second graders. First of all, the neighborhood block in which the story occurs is a "salad bowl," tossing together races, cultures, and age groups. Also, Rosa's extended family gives readers a glimpse of a non-traditional lifestyle they might not otherwise encounter. The characters cope with difficulties (an out-of-work father, separated parents, etc.) that many youngsters today also face.

Additionally, the author packs her story with a range of emotions similar to feelings many children routinely have. Rosa bursts with excitement, pride, and satisfaction; she tingles with anticipation; she also hurts from worry and stage-fright. Rosa, her family, and friends never shrink from their feelings, but deal with them constructively.

Music, Music for Everyone adds an affective dimension to any study of "neighborhood." The book's difficult readability, however, might prevent some young readers from grasping its important lessons. Consequently, teachers should deliver the story in a whole-class, read-aloud session with pre-post reading discussion.

Developing Communication Skills

The author introduces several aspects of non-verbal communication in the course of the story. Read the book to students, then use the following activities to explore these modes of communication.

1. Reread for children the passage in which Rosa describes her house as "so empty and so quiet" (about 10 pages into the story). Examine the illustrations that precede this passage; ask children to list elements of these pictures that communicate this message even more effectively than the words. Then, ask children the following questions to prompt discussion:
    a. Do the pictures communicate the same feelings as the words?
    b. What do the pictures make you feel?

c. What things in the pictures communicate these feelings better?
d. Do pictures or words communicate these feelings better?
e. What types of things do pictures "tell" better than words?

To extend this activity, have students choose one feeling and draw a picture that communicates it. Share these pictures with the class.

2. Reread the description of the Oak Street Band's party performance. Focus discussion on the emotional reactions to the girls' music. Ask children to talk about favorite music and the feelings that these songs generate.

Bring at least three different types of music to class. Songs might express joy, sadness, military or national pride, love, etc. Play each genre and then ask children to write just one word that best expresses his/her reaction. Compare reactions after each genre.

Have children bring their favorite music to class. Have children write sentences/paragraphs about the feelings being expressed.

Nurturing the Affective Domain

After reading the story aloud, show children the illustrations near the end of the book that depict neighbors dancing to the music of the Oak Street Band. Guide children to the observation that the musicians appear different from each other and the dancers are a similarly diverse group. List ways in which band members and party guests differ physically (in terms of age, race, clothing, hairstyles, etc.); discuss with children whether or not these differences are really significant (i.e., Do they prevent these people from having fun? Do they prevent these people from talking?).

Finally, have children name characteristics that the people share. Guide children to the conclusion that these similarities outweigh any physical differences these people might have. Take photos of your diverse (red hair, etc., may be considered a "diverse" characteristic in your class) students engaged in school and classroom activities during a week or two. Select committees of 3 or 4 students to label a few of the photos with a sentence expressing a feeling which the photo emits.

Promoting
Thinking Skills

The story suggests activities that build two key aspects of reflective thinking—decision-making and time-order sequencing.

1. Read the story to the children and establish its major happenings. Divide the class into pairs; have each pair draw a picture of one of these key events. Then let the class construct a timeline from these drawings. Use the timeline to support generalizations about cause-effect relationships between these events.

2. After reading the story to children, review the problems that confronted Rosa's family (Grandma sick, Mama working and caring for her, the money jar emptying, etc.). Talk about this situation briefly. Brainstorm courses of action that Rosa and her family might have taken to resolve their problems; list these options on the chalkboard or overhead. Divide children into small groups (3-4 per group); have each group select the "best" alternative and cooperatively write a paragraph justifying its choice. To conclude the activity, have the groups share their decisions, then briefly discuss the pros and cons of each option.

Using Map and
Globe Skills

After reading the story aloud and establishing its main events, focus discussion on the business operated by Leora's mother. Be sure that children understand the notion of a "corner market;" compare/contrast this store with the "super market" that children might find more familiar. Follow this discussion with these activities.

1. Advise children that they are business people interested in building a neighborhood market in your town. Discuss factors that influence the location of a foodstore. Use a town map to consider possible sites for the new market. Reach a class consensus on the best place to build and mark it on the map.

2. To follow up the previous activity, provide children with dittoed outlines of their new market building. Have them (working individually, in pairs, or in small groups) "map" proposed floorplans for the store. Let children share their efforts with the class.

3. Help the class determine the closest market to your school. Then, children (working singly, paired, or in groups) draw maps of the best route to take from the school to the store.

Practicing
Social Interaction

Music, Music for Everyone presents several opportunities in which children may work together in groups.

1. After reading the story to children, take a field trip to a local supermarket. Prepare children in advance to look for examples of productive group behavior during the visit. After the trip, have children list the departments that comprised the supermarket. Then, discuss two dimensions of positive interaction at work in the store: people working together within each department and departments cooperating to make the store profitable.

2. Read the story to children and discuss the Oak Street Band. Then organize a class band using simple instruments and prerecorded background music. After some practice, the "musicians" may give a recital for schoolmates and/or family members.

3. After a read-aloud session, discuss the story's characters with children. Pay particular attention to Grandma and Mama. Divide children into small groups. Have each group consider the names that Rosa called these important people in her life. Ask the groups to list the different names that members call their grandmothers and mothers. Share these lists in a large group setting. Conclude the activity by talking about the origin of some of these names.

CHAPTER FIFTEEN

I Know a Lady
by Charlotte Zolotow

Among the NCSS's "Notable Trade Books in the Social Studies" in 1984.

Spache Readability Level—4 +
Fry Readability Level—6

Zolotow, Charlotte. *I Know a Lady*. Pictures by James Stevenson. New York: Greenwillow Books, 1984. Unpaged (approx. 24 pages). ISBN 0-688-03837-9 and 0-688-03838-7 (library binding).

   Zolotow packs a story that grabs any reader's heart into the confines of this short book. Sally has a special friend—an "old lady" who lives on her block. This lady shows how much she cares by knowing the names of all the neighborhood children, baking treats for them at the holidays, and watching out for cats, birds, and dogs. Sally loves her older friend. She loves her so much that, one day, she might well become the same sort of special "old lady" in her neighborhood!.

Relationship to Social Studies

Zolotow and Stevenson make a productive team. The author's rambling style and the illustrator's whimiscal sketches convey many important lessons for any second grader studying "neighborhood." Children might compare/contrast the book's calm, small town setting with the faster-paced neighborhoods in which many youngsters now live. More importantly, the story's characters model a relationship seldom seen today—a sharing, caring interchange between young and old people. This story can help teach children that older people can be so much more than nursing home inmates.

Zolotow and Stevenson craft a work, moreover, that suggests skill-building experiences for second grade social studies students. The thinking and map and globe areas seem particularly promising.

I Know a Lady has a simple, direct plot that primary children will find engaging and understandable. Yet, its involved sentence structure and advanced vocabulary might defeat all but the most able second grade readers. The story is better delivered to students in read-aloud fashion.

Developing Communication Skills

Zolotow extensively treats the ways in which people communicate their caring to others in *I Know a Lady*. The book introduces several activities that explore this theme.

1. Read the story aloud, then talk about the relationship between the "old lady" and Sally. Focus discussion on an interesting fact: the woman clearly communicates to neighborhood children that she cares for them, yet, never once says, "I care for you." Examine the ways in which the "old lady" transmits this message without ever having to say it. To extend the activity, the class can pick a school staff member for whom **they** care a lot (a cook, another teacher, an aide, **etc.) an**d brainstorm ways to communicate their feelings without having to say them. Over a week's time, let the class try their ideas on this special person.

2. Read the story and discuss its central rela-

tionship with children. Ask volunteers to describe someone they care for as much as Sally loved the "old lady." Then, provide time for all students to reflect about someone that they truly care for; have each child write a letter to this person expressing feelings for him/her. Once the letters are "polished," children may deliver or mail them to their special persons if distances prevent a visit.

Nurturing the Affective Domain

After reading the story to the class, implement one of the following activities that encourage students to form a friendship with an older person similar to the one Sally enjoyed with the "old lady."

1. With children's input, select an older neighborhood resident(s) that your class might "adopt" for a semester. Invite this person(s) to visit your classroom. Provide time for class members to visit him/her/them individually or in small groups. Finally, encourage students to help this class friend with home projects whenever possible (raking leaves, shoveling snow, weeding, etc.). From time to time, discuss with children how this relationship makes them feel.

2. Arrange for your students to become "penpals" with elderly patients at a nursing home or care facility in your town. A student committee or parent volunteers can deliver letters from school to nursing home and vice versa. As the letter-writing continues, discuss how students feel as a result of it.

Promoting Thinking Skills

Zolotow's brief narrative covers a surprising length of time—almost an entire year. The following activities utilize this time-frame to build student's sequencing skills.

1. Read the story to children, then have them list seasons mentioned in the story. Discuss descriptions that the author uses for each season (particularly the flowers). Then divide children into four small groups; assign each group a season. Have each group gather "stuff" representative of its season (photos, pressed flowers, sports equipment, clothing, etc.). Use the items that the groups col-

lect to construct a time-line display showing the seasons in proper order.

2. Read the story aloud, then list the holidays that the author references. Brainstorm other major holidays that Zolotow omitted. Add holidays reflecting various cultures/ethnic groups to this list (Martin Luther King Day, Yom Kippur, the Chinese New Year, etc.). Then have students research dates for the holidays on your final list. Finally, construct a time-line that sequences these holidays and display it in the classroom.

Using Map and Globe Skills

After the story has been read aloud and thoroughly discussed by the class, consider implementing the following activities that build students' awareness of maps and spatial relationships.

1. Assign students a task: to closely observe the illustrations and carefully listen to words that provide information about the neighborhood in which the "old lady" and Sally lived. Then, reread the story to the class. Briefly discuss maps and their functions; stress the notion that maps give a "bird's-eye view" of an area. Divide children into small groups (3 students per group); have each group make a map of Sally's block on a transparency.

These maps should approximate the one shown at the end of the chapter.

Provide time for groups to share their maps on an overhead projector. To extend this activity, let the groups retell sections of the story using their maps as visual aids.

2. Ask children to think about an older family friend or relative—who this person is, what he/she looks like, and where this person lives. Then, pair students and have the partners take turns giving each other directions to this person's house. To extend this activity, have children translate these directions into simple maps.

Practicing Social Interaction

After reading the story to children, discuss the treats that the "old lady" made for her young friends and list them on the chalkboard or overhead. Tell students that the class will enjoy these treats on special occasions just like the story's characters. Over the school year, form committees of parents and students to plan holiday parties. Remind these groups of the appropriate treat for the party they are planning. At each party, as the treats are served, remind the entire class where the idea for those treats came from and briefly discuss why the "old lady" might have selected them for Sally and her friends. If you tried the penpal activity ("Nurturing the Affective Domain," Activity 2), invite the penpals to these parties and share the secret behind the choice of treats. You might take a party to the nursing home if the penpals health prevents them from visiting the school.

SALLY'S NEIGHBORHOOD

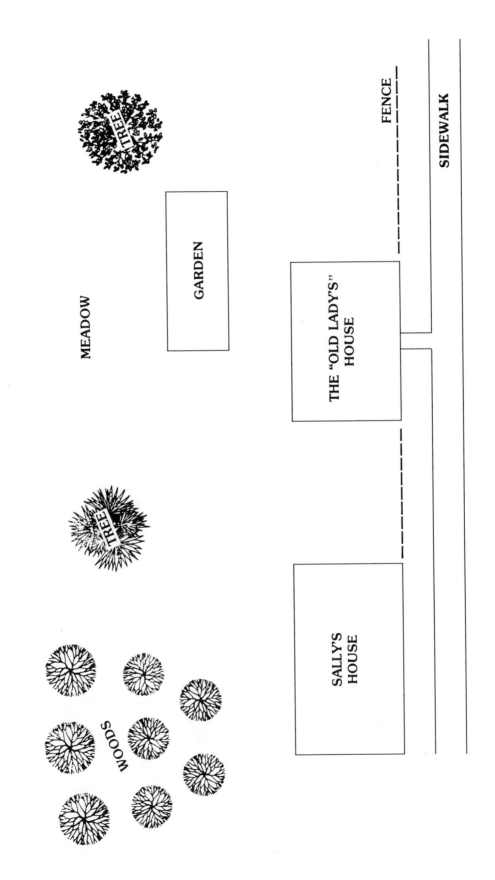

CHAPTER SIXTEEN

The Town Mouse and the Country Mouse
retold and illustrated by
Lorinda Bryan Cauley

Listed among "Notable Trade Books in the Social Studies" in 1984,
and honored as a "Children's Choices" selection the following year.

Spache Readability Level—4+
Fry Readability Level—6

Cauley, Lorinda Bryan. ***The Town Mouse and the Country Mouse***. New York: G. P. Putnam's Sons, 1984. Unpaged (approx. 32 pages). ISBN 0-399-21123-3 and 0-399-21126-8 (paperback).

Cauley's naturalistic drawings spice her retelling of a classic tale in which the characters learn that life is not always greener in the other fellow's yard. The Country Mouse lived simply and comfortably in a hollow log he called home. Country Mouse enjoyed his pastoral life until a relative paid a visit. Town Mouse loudly informed his country cousin that rural living was too boring, demanding, and crude for anyone of refinement and taste. Persuaded that perhaps his existence was not all he thought, Country Mouse decided to try city life. At first, Town Mouse's home dazzled his rustic cousin; the lavish furnishings and rich food (left-over from a human meal) tempted County Mouse. Terrifying encounters with servants, a small child, and ferocious dogs quickly convinced Country Mouse that he belonged in a safer, more restful environment. Before Country Mouse left, the cousins exchanged invitations for return visits sometime in the future. Such visits likely never happen, though, as both cousins had become convinced that there really was no place like home!.

Relationship to Social Studies

Cauley's version of this city-country fable holds visual and stylistic appeal for children. Though an enticing work, the book's vocabulary, sentence structure, and complex theme might be too much of a challenge for third grade readers. Teachers are advised to prepare youngsters with pre-reading activities, to read the book aloud to a group of students, and to then extensively discuss its difficult ideas.

While demanding, *The Town Mouse and the Country Mouse* contributes much to any third grade social studies program. The book, first of all, allows students to compare/contrast two distinct examples of "community"—rural and urban. Cauley's work also shows children that individuals can hold divergent views and different lifestyles, yet still respect and care for one another. Finally, the book provides content for social studies skill-building activities, particularly in the thinking and map & globe areas.

Developing Communication Skills

A key happening and the nature of the story itself introduce activities that allow children to explore two aspects of communication.

1. Read the story aloud, then ask how Town Mouse came to visit his country cousin (Country Mouse invited him by letter). Encourage children to speculate on the contents of this invitation. Point out to children that whatever Country Mouse wrote, he did not communicate effectively. The city cousin misunderstood his country cousin's circumstances and, as a result, had an awful visit.

Then, divide the class in half. One half assumes the role of Country Mouse and writes letters inviting their "city cousin" for a visit; the other half becomes Town Mouse and drafts acceptances of this invitation. Review passages from the book describing the cousins' lifestyles; have children include this information in their letters to avoid the misunderstandings in the story. Take time to share selected letters. Use these examples to generate discussion of ways in which effective communication reduces unpleasant surprises like the ones that the cousins' encountered.

2. *The Town Mouse and the Country Mouse* is an updating of an ancient story form—the fable. After reading the book to children, explain fables briefly. Your librarian might help you find an alternate version of the story in *Aesop's Fables*; share this and other fables with the class. Discuss common elements that these tales share with Cauley's work (animals with human characteristics, sudden twists of plot, a moral lesson, etc.). When children grasp the essentials of a fable, have each student write one of their own. Provide a common moral for these stories; make it a lesson to which children can relate (e.g. "true friendship lasts through any adversity"). To conclude this activity, share, discuss, and then display these fables.

Nurturing the Affective Domain

Read the story aloud and establish its major events with children. Then, talk about the sometimes negative interactions between the cousins; the two mice said some nasty things about each other. Review these dialogues with the class. Ask children if feelings were hurt. Decide which cousin used the bluntest and most destructive language (the Town Mouse). Follow discussion with one of the following activities (or both if time permits).

1. Choose a particularly negative conversation between the cousins and reread it to students. Briefly discuss ways in which the cousins might have interacted without being so harsh. Divide students into pairs; instruct the pairs to role play this interchange substituting positive language for the cousins' blunt words. Conclude the activity by discussing ways in which these new versions might lead to improved relations between the cousins.

2. Extend the above discussion into the relationship between honesty and hurt feelings. Ask children:
   a. Was Town Mouse being honest and direct with his cousin?
   b. Did this honesty hurt his cousin's feelings?
   c. Might he have been less honest in expressing his views?
   d. Is it dishonest to "hold back" to spare feelings? Why? Why not?

Promoting Thinking Skills

After reading the story to the class, review the descriptions of the ways in which the mouse cousins lived. Reread key passages; question students until they have a thorough understanding of each lifestyle. Then, compare/contrast these modes of living with students; record columns of "similarities" and "differences" between the lifestyles on a chalkboard or overhead. Next, compare/contrast these situations with the way of life in your community. Help children determine which lifestyle most resembles their own and support their decision.

To extend this activity, have each child fold a large sheet of construction paper in half. On one half, the student makes a collage of newspaper and magazine photos showing an urban lifestyle today; on the other, he/she creates a "rural living" collage. Then, have each student write a response to the question, "Which lifestyle (rural or urban) do you prefer and why?" Conclude by listing advantages and disadvantages of these lifestyles; display the collages and responses on a wall or bulletin board.

Using Map and Globe Skills

The book suggests activities that build awareness of how location affects inhabitants and promotes students' ability to construct simple maps.

1. Read the story aloud, then focus students' attention on illustrations that show the areas in which the two mice lived. Generate characteristics that these places demonstrated (i.e. "the Town Mouse's home was surrounded by paved roads"). Then, discuss ways in which the location where each mouse lived infuenced the *ways* in which he lived. If time permits, brainstorm a list of characteristics for your community's location and discuss how they influence the ways in which class members live.

2. After a read-aloud session, show the illustrations depicting where the cousin's homes were located; discuss the major features of these areas with children. Divide the class into small groups (about 3 children in each); randomly assign each group the task of mapping the Town Mouse's area or the Country Mouse's home. Establish with children essential features that these maps should have (such as: a simple key, use of color, and accurate representation of the relationships between key features). Share the finished maps; discuss differences/similarities between these two areas and between these areas and your community.

Practicing Social Interaction

The book introduces a number of experiences that allow children to interact productively. These activities include:

1. Read the story to children and discuss its major events. At a later date, take a class trip to a setting markedly different than the one in which most students live (e.g. if your school is in town, visit a farm). Before the trip, divide students into pairs. Have one partner look for ways the field trip site differs from his/her home environment; have the other partner observe the site for similarities. On the bus trip home, the pairs may discuss their findings and report the results of their interaction to the entire class.

2. After reading the story aloud, discuss the foods that the Town Mouse and the Country Mouse consumed. Discuss which of these dishes might be served at a class lunch; reach a consensus on dishes from the story that would comprise a menu for this event. Next, divide students into small groups. Have some groups prepare menu items; one group can accompany you on an expedition to the supermarket to purchase food; appoint another group as servers; assign one group the task of selecting and inviting some "special guests" to the lunch. All children should share "clean-up" duties. After the gala meal, discuss ways in which cooperation assisted class efforts and times that it broke-down to the detriment of all.

CHAPTER SEVENTEEN

Miss Rumphius
by Barbara Cooney

Winner of the American Book Award and an IRA/CBC "Children's Choices" book in 1983; also, nominated for the Golden Sower Award (Nebraska) in 1984-1985.

Spache Readability Level—4+
Fry Readability Level—6

Cooney, Barbara. **Miss Rumphius**. New York: The Viking Press, 1982. Unpaged (approx. 32 pages). ISBN 0-670-47958-6.

Cooney captures a memorable woman's indomitable spirit and quest to beautify her world. Little Alice narrates the saga of her Great-aunt Alice Rumphius—world traveler, story-teller, and bringer of beauty. Grandfather left Miss Rumphius three goals—journey far, return to a home by the sea, and make the world more beautiful. When she grew older, Miss Rumphius journeyed to a tropical island, safaried jungles, climbed mountains, and trekked deserts. A sudden injury told her it was time to retire to a home by the sea. After awhile, she began reflecting on her third goal. By chance, some lupine seeds she once planted grew about her land. Struck by their beauty, Miss Rumphius spread many more seeds around town and earned the title, the Lupine Lady.

Now very, very old, Miss Rumphius sits in her cottage and tells Little Alice and her friends of faraway places and the need for beauty. One day, Little Alice leaves her great-aunt convinced that she too will travel and live by the sea; she does wonder about just one thing—how will she make the world a more beautiful place?

Relationship to Social Studies

Miss Rumphius contains a wealth of social studies lessons for third grade students. The book, first of all, introduces young readers to an unforgettable character who models important citizenship qualities. Alice Rumphius works to leave her community better than she found it. She persists in her mission despite taunts from some neighbors. Like any good citizen, moreover, she dedicates her life to learning more about her world.

Secondly, Alice Rumphius refuses to permit convention to handicap or frustrate her. She accomplishes things that a woman is not supposed to try. She remains her own person into her twilight years. Children today need role models with such conviction and purpose.

The story's readability level and sophisticated ideas place it beyond the reach of all but the most able third grade readers. When read aloud, however, the book contributes to a study of "community."

Developing Communication Skills

Read the book to children. Then implement the following writing activities that boost students' abilities to communicate key ideas and interesting information.

1. Ask children to consider what a person's name communicates about him or her. Review the various names that the title character receives in the course of the story. Discuss with children what these names/nicknames tell others about Miss Rumphius. Consider whether they communicate bad or good things about her; help students determine what constitutes an effective nickname. Have each child select a classmate, a person in your school, or a community "celebrity" that they admire. Then, each student writes a paragraph that includes:

    a. a nickname for this person that captures his/her most positive trait, and

    b. reasons why this nickname is appropriate. Provide time for students

to share their paragraphs with the class and with their nicknamed persons.

2. Divide students into small groups (3 per group) and let each team select one of the many unusual topics referenced in Cooney's story (such as: ship figureheads, cigar store Indians, lupines, a conservatory, etc.). After thorough research, the groups prepare written reports on their topics; encourage them to supplement their summaries with visual aids (i.e. maps, pictures, diagrams, models, etc.). If time permits, the groups may share their reports with the class before submitting them to you.

Nurturing the Affective Domain

Miss Rumphius's third goal, making the world more beautiful, introduces experiences that heighten students' sense of commitment.

1. Read the story aloud. Discuss Alice Rumphius's desire to increase the beauty of her world and the way in which she achieved this goal. Examine the book's final page with students. Note that, although Miss Rumphius transmits her mission to her grand-niece, Little Alice lacks a means for achieving this end. Brainstorm how Little Alice might make her world a lovelier place. Have children draw a picture, make a model, or construct a diorama depicting one of the projects that Little Alice might try. Display these artworks when they are completed.

2. After reading the story to students, discuss Miss Rumphius's third goal. Ask children if they know of anyone like Miss Rumphius who has tried to make the world a more beautiful place. Let volunteers share these examples. Have children scour newspapers and magazines for photographic examples of citizens who work to beautify their surroundings. Children may create collages from these pictures and share them with the class. Display these creations when finished.

3. Emphasize the fact that beauty can be found and enhanced in *everyday* life at school and at home. Select walls of a classroom, corridor, etc. in school that could stand some beautification. Divide the class into groups to come up with plans for beautification projects. Implement these plans.

Promoting
Critical Thinking

The involved plot and rich vocabulary of *Miss Rumphius* suggest opportunities for students to think on a "higher level." First, read the book aloud and discuss its main events. Then, in the following activities, students brainstorm a variety of lists and use them to develop their abilities to compare/contrast and classify information.

1.   Let students brainstorm a list of the many "communities" in which Alice Rumphius visited or lived. Then, discuss how these locations differed, but also shared some common features. Have each student select the community in which he/she would most like to live. Have students write paragraphs supporting their choices.

2.   On the chalkboard or overhead, write three categories of things that appear in Cooney's story (possibilities include: "places," "animals," "strange objects," "beautiful things," "people," and "buildings"). Select a passage from the story and reread it for children. As you encounter each item named in the passage, ask children if it belongs in one of the three categories and, if so, which one. Repeat this exercise with categories suggested by your students.

3.   Generate a list of "strange" items mentioned in the story (i.e. tall ships, cigar store Indians, cockatoos, the Lotus Eaters, etc.). After they have reflected on this list, ask children:

   a. Have you ever seen these items Miss Rumphius encountered?
   b. Was Miss Rumphius's world similar or different from ours? How?

Using Map and
Globe Skills

Miss Rumphius's travels suggest many activities that encourage students to apply geographic skills.

Two possibilities are listed below.

1.   Read the story aloud, then establish a chronology of the title character's journeys. Divide students into small groups and provide each group with a world map. Assign each group the task of charting a route that Miss Rumphius might have taken. Let the groups share their efforts with the class.

2.   Brainstorm a list of the places that Miss Rumphius visited (a city by the sea, tall mountains, a tropical island, etc.) and record it on the chalkboard or overhead. Using world maps in their social studies texts as a resource, have students find two or three examples of each location Miss Rumphius toured. If time permits, encourage students to learn more about some of the places they found in their textbooks and report their information to the class.

Practicing
Social Interaction

After reading the story aloud, talk about its main ideas with students. Gradually focus discussion on the goals that Miss Rumphius worked so hard to achieve. Pay particular attention to her third goal—leaving her world more beautiful than she found it. Leave students with the conclusion that this goal is a worthy one that the class might adopt. Consider ways in which the class might share Miss Rumphius's life-long goal of leaving her surroundings more beautiful than she found them. Generate a list of projects the class might undertake to improve their school's outside appearance. Help the class choose one or two of these projects that are "do-able." Organize students into committees to accomplish these tasks. After their completion, discuss with students how these efforts made them feel.

CHAPTER EIGHTEEN

How My Parents Learned to Eat
by Ina R. Friedman

The recipient of the Christopher Award and a
"Notable Children's Trade Books in the Social Studies" selection in 1984.

Spache Readability Level—4+
Fry Readability Level—3

Friedman, Ina R. *How My Parents Learned to Eat*. Illustrated by Allen Say. Boston: Houghton Mifflin Company, 1984. 32 pages. ISBN 0-395-35379-3.

In this lighthearted tale, cultural misunderstandings abound as a young girl explains why her family eats sometimes with chopsticks and sometimes with knives and forks. The young narrator details her parents' courtship in Japan. Everyday, her father, John, an American sailor, and her mother, Aiko, a Japanese schoolgirl, walked and enjoyed each other's company. But they were afraid to share a meal because silverware baffled Aiko and chopsticks frustrated John.

Finally, John learned of his impending transfer and decided to ask Aiko to marry him. After a crash course at a Japanese restaurant, he was ready to tackle chopsticks and invited Aiko to dinner. Embarrassed, Aiko consulted an uncle, who taught her the mechanics of silverware as he learned them in England. The couple chose a Western restaurant. After watching her for some time, John finally asked Aiko where she had learned to eat in such an unusual way. After hearing Aiko's story, John explained that English and American eating habits were very different. The couple chuckled at their silliness and concluded that "chopsticks versus cutlery" would never be an issue after they were married.

Relationship to Social Studies

Friedman and Say's work adds a multicultural dimension to any third grade social studies program. The book portrays life in a community that differs greatly from the one in which most Americans dwell. The characters, moreover, model multicultural understanding for young readers; they acknowledge conflicting customs, but refuse to let them interfere with feelings for each other.

How My Parents Learned to Eat also provides opportunities for children to practice a variety of social studies skills. The setting introduces activities that promote geographic competency; the characters' language differences suggest experiences that boost children's communication skills.

Besides being a valuable supplement to social studies instruction, the book is interesting and fairly readable for most third graders. The story can be read by individual or small groups of students as well as read aloud.

Developing Communication Skills

John and Aiko struggled with communication problems caused by different cultural backgrounds. Their example introduces activities in which children examine the difficult "art" of communicating across cultures.

1. Read the story to children and review its main events. Focus attention on the fact that John and Aiko seem to understand each other well, despite speaking different languages. To prompt discussion, ask children:
    a. Did John and Aiko communicate in English or Japanese? Why so?
    b. Did they have other ways of communicating besides language? Explain.
    c. How would you have communicated if you were John or Aiko?
2. After reading the book aloud, discuss the communication difficulties that John and Aiko might have faced initially. Have volunteers role play the couple's first encounter; instruct the role play-

ers to emphasize non-verbal modes of communication in their exchange. Discuss the role play, particularly how communication difficulties made the players feel and the most effective ways in which they overcame these problems.

3. Read and discuss the story with children. Then, introduce the class to Japanese words that John and Aiko might have used during their courtship. If possible, invite a Japanese speaker to model oral and written language for the class.

Nurturing the Affective Domain

How My Parents Learned to Eat offers many opportunities to further the multicultural understanding of third grade youngsters. Read the story aloud, then implement the following activities.

1. Advise students that the story illustrates a cultural truism—people in Japan and America have different eating habits and favorite foods. Draw examples of these differences from the story. Then, expand the discussion to other countries; compare/contrast the diets of these cultures with American eating habits and foods. Ask children why people around the world eat different foods in different ways. Guide children to the conclusion that diet is not arbitrarily or whimsically determined. Rather, a number of factors (climate, religion, technology, etc.) determine what people eat and how they eat it. End the lesson with examples supporting this observation.

2. Discuss how foods from other cultures has influenced the American diet. Generate a list on chalkboard or overhead of foods imported to America that we commonly eat. (Be careful, however, not to include truly American foods like pizza or chop suey on this list). Use colored pins to locate where these foods came from on a world map; make some generalizations about where these foods originated. Point out how these "imports" have enriched the American diet considerably. Then list restaurants in your community that serve "foreign" foods. If possible, take the class to eat at one; if not, have a small group of student volunteers visit a restaurant and report to the class.

3. Begin with the assumption that the American diet has been enriched by foods from many cultures. Then consider an interesting proposition—has America returned the favor by "ex-

porting" foods? Let children brainstorm what these foods might be. Provide students with examples of foods that America has indeed "exported" (hot-dog, hamburger, milkshake, etc.)

Promoting Critical Thinking

After children have read and discussed the story, consider these activities in which students compare/contrast information.

1. On an opaque projector, show children the story's first and last pages for approximately one minute each. Divide the students into small groups (3 per group). Have half the groups brainstorm written lists of details from the opening picture; assign the other half the task of recording what they remember from the final picture. Provide time for the groups to share their lists with the entire class; combine these efforts into class lists detailing the two pictures. With these class lists as resources, have children compare/contrast the two eating styles that these drawings portray.

2. Over several days, have small groups of students examine the pictures in the story and generate two lists—items they might find in their hometown and items they would not find. In a large group session, let the groups share their lists. Use them to note similarities and differences between life in Aiko's Japan and your area.

Using Map and Globe Skills

Once the book has been read to students, its setting introduces a number of activities in which children utilize map and globe skills.

1. On both a globe and a world map, have small groups of children locate the U.S. and Japan. Let them discover neighbors of both countries. Have them find the approximate location of their community and the community in which Aiko lived (Yokohama). Conclude with students comparing/contrasting Japan and the U.S. in terms of size, shape, landforms, and location. To extend this activity, help students determine the distance between the two countries and the flying time between them.

2. Have students search magazines and newspapers for photos of life in Japan. Combine these visuals with maps of Japan to create a class bulletin board — "Our East Asian Neighbor."

3. Expose students to "living" examples of Japanese culture. Invite a guest speaker to talk to students about daily life in Japan. Show slides or photos of this Asian country. Share Japanese food with children. Allow them to eat a meal with chopsticks. Show students Japanese clothing, art, and household items; play Japanese music.

Practicing Social Interaction

The activities below divide class projects into a series of tasks that students complete in small groups or with their families.

1. Read the story to students. Discuss their knowledge of Aiko's homeland. Point out to students how little they know about a country increasingly important to the U.S. Divide students into small groups (3-4 per group). Have each group write a letter requesting information about Japan from a potential source (these might include: the Japanese Embassy in Washington, D.C., the nearest Japanese consulate, the American Embassy in Japan, the East Asia Society, an Asian Studies department at a nearby university, a Japanese business, etc.). As responses are received, allow the appropriate small group to inspect the results of its inquiry. Organize the information into a vertical file that the class can use to learn more about Japan.

2. Read the story to students and discuss what it reveals about Japanese life. Assign students some "homework" — with the help of their parents, they will list all the Japanese products they can find at home. The next day, divide the class into small groups (4-5 students each). Give each group a worksheet like the one shown at the end of the chapter.

Have the groups place items from each member's home list in the appropriate category on the worksheet. In a large group discussion, guide students to the conclusion that Japan and the U.S. are increasingly interdependent economically. Help them make judgments about the types of products for which we depend upon Japan.

THE MANY TYPES OF JAPANESE PRODUCTS

For homework, each member of your group listed Japanese products found at home. Now, group each item from your list in the right category below.

ENTERTAINMENT	TRANSPORTATION	KITCHEN APPLIANCE

SPORTS	FURNITURE	CLOTHING

74

CHAPTER NINETEEN

Katie Morag and the Two Grandmothers
by Mairi Hedderwick

Included on the 1986 listing of "Notable Children's Trade Books in the Social Studies."

Spache Readability Level—4 +
Fry Readability Level—5

Hedderwick, Mairi. *Katie Morag and the Two Grandmothers*. Boston: Little, Brown and Company, 1985. Unpaged (approx. 32 pages). ISBN 0-316-35400-7 and 0-316-35400-7 (library binding).

Hedderwick sets a traditional tale of "victory snatched from defeat" in an unusual location peopled by characters bordering on the eccentric. Katie Morag lives on the Isle of Struay, off the British coast, with her parents, Mr. and Mrs. McColl. Her two grandmothers contrast sharply: "no-nonsense" Grannie Island raises sheep and sails a fishing boat while Granma Mainland wears frilly dresses and perfects her appearance. Neither has much use for the other until a near-catastrophe strikes.

Ignoring the arrival of Show Day, Grannie Island's prize sheep, Alecina muddies herself apparently beyond repair. Grannie despairs that Alecina can ever get clean enough to retain her championship until Katie Morag remembers her other grandmother's hair whitener. After a good wash and several doses of Granma Mainland's conditioner, Alecina wins yet another blue ribbon. The victory has two results. For a long time, Grannie Island and Katie smile at their cleverness and Grannie never belittles Granma again.

Relationship to Social Studies

Katie Morag relates to social studies instruction in a variety of ways. First of all, the book acquaints third graders with a strange, island community that they can compare/contrast with their own. Secondly, Hedderwick introduces students to unique individuals who live non-traditional lifestyles. Several of these characters, moreover, find mutual interests after years of distrust. Their transition from jealousy to acceptance is a model from which children can profit. Additionally, the book suggests activities that promote thinking, geography, and communication skills.

Hedderwick's humor and odd characters should hold children's interest well. Her writing style and choice of setting make it a difficult book that is best delivered to students as read-aloud selection.

Developing Communication Skills

The book's richly detailed illustrations communicate as much of the story line as the text. Hedderwick's skillful use of pictures to tell much of her tale suggests lessons in which children explore visual means of communication. Read the story to the class, discuss its main events, and implement one or more of the following such activities.

1. Select a two-page illustration that evoked a positive response during the read-aloud session. Examine this visual in depth with students. Ask them to consider the following questions:
   a. What things are happening in this picture? Describe them.
   b. What does this picture tell you about life on Struay?
   c. What does it communicate about the story's main characters?

2. Focus student's attention on the many signs that are part of Hedderwick's illustrations. Examine these signs; categorize them by type (i.e. "labels," "nameplates," "posters," etc.). Discuss the information they provide. Then, take a walking tour of the school; after returning to the classroom, list and type the signs the class observed. Consider what they communicated about life in your building.

3. Have students (individually or in pairs) make signs that communicate classroom life to an "outsider." These signs might be directional, informational, or personal. To conclude the activity, post these signs and discuss the information they provide.

Nurturing the Affective Domain

The relationship between Katie Morag's two grandmothers affords children opportunity to examine feelings of "distrust" and how to most effectively overcome them. Read the story to children and discuss the interactions between major characters. Focus on the way in which Grannie Island and Granma Mainland get along.

Establish their true feelings for one another and decide on a term to define their relationship (perhaps "distrust" or "dislike"). Determine whether these negative feelings are shared or come mainly from one direction. Brainstorm reasons why this relationship is so icy. Guide children to the observation that different backgrounds cause their feelings; rural Grannie Island distrusts the "city ways" of Granma Mainland. Finally, examine the events that thawed the "Cold War" between the two women. Discuss other ways in which the grandmothers' relationship might have been improved.

If time permits, let volunteers present "case studies" of people they know who dislike/distrust each other for the same reasons that Grannie Island and Granma Mainland disagree. Discourage the use of names in these descriptions. Have the class brainstorm ways in which these "real-life" relationships might be improved.

Promoting Critical Thinking

After reading the story aloud, present children with the following opportunities for decision-making/problem-solving.

1. Have students, working in discussion groups, wrestle with the story's setting. First of all, each group should decide if the story occurred in the United States and substantiate its conclusion with evidence drawn from the book (data support-

ing a "NO" position can be found by examining the clothing, machinery, signs, geography, and language used throughout the book). To extend this activity, the groups may become detectives, "tracking down" the place in which *Katie Morag* happened, and substantiating their hypothesis (probably off the Scottish coast from the language, place names, and clothing).

2. Pair students and have them assume the identities of Katie Morag and Grannie Island. Reread the passages describing the problem these characters faced (a stubborn and dirty Alecina). Have each pair role play the way in which it would have solved this crisis.

Using Map and Globe Skills

The "picture map" shown in the book's flyleaf introduces two activities that increase students' knowledge of map-making.

1. Read the story to students, then examine the "picture map" with them. Discuss what information the map provides the reader (the topography of Struay, knowledge of the island's people and architecture, etc.). Consider what information this type of map does *not* provide very well (i.e. could a visitor easily find Grannie Island's home with this map?). Use this discussion to make the transition between "picture maps" and "overview maps" for children. If time permits, have small groups convert this map into a standard or ("bird's-eye-view") map of the island and share their efforts with the class.

2. Read the story aloud and discuss the "picture map" with children. Divide students into small groups; have each group construct a similar map of the area surrounding your school. Share these maps with the class; discuss the strengths and weaknesses of this type of map with children.

Practicing Social Interaction

Katie Morag suggests two major projects that provide ample opportunity for students to interact productively in group settings.

1. Read the story aloud and help students establish just what a "Show Day" is. Examine illustrations closely and list things that the people of Struay did on this special day. Then, begin planning a class version of Show Day. Assign the major planning tasks to small groups of students. These tasks might include: refreshments, advertising, determining show rules and categories, prizes, invitations for special guests, and scheduling of whom will exhibit what. After your Show Day is over, discuss factors that made events go smoothly, problems that arose, and ways in which these difficulties were best eliminated.

2. Read the story aloud and discuss its main events briefly. Then, tell students that the story occurred in Great Britain; to better appreciate this interesting land, the class will take a "field trip" to England, Ireland, Scotland, and Wales. Plan experiences for children that simulate a 2-week trip around Britain. Show films, invite guest speakers, prepare English dishes, display British products, hang posters and photos on the walls—any experience that will immerse students in the British way of life.

Additionally, provide activities that simulate travel abroad (i.e. a passport for each "traveler," an imaginary plane ride, checking through Customs, etc.). Use small groups of students to complete the more mechanical tasks needed for this project (i.e. stapling passports or rearranging chairs). When students have "returned" from their British "trip," thoroughly review what they learned.

CHAPTER TWENTY

Round Trip
by Ann Jonas

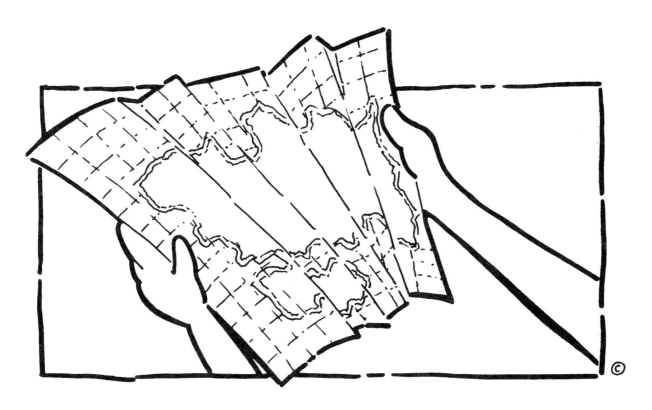

Distinguished by honors that include: listing among the New York *Times'* "Best Illustrated Children's Trade Books in the Social Studies" in 1983; selection as an IRA/CBC "Children's Choices" books for 1984; and winner of the Golden Sower (Nebraska) Award in 1985.

Spache Readability Level—4+
Fry Readability Level—2

Jonas, Ann. **Round Trip**. New York: Greenwillow Books, 1983. Unpaged (approx. 32 pages). ISBN 0-688-01722-X and 0-688-01781-9 (library binding).

The author's "reversible" illustrations place her work among the most fascinating travelogues ever written. Held "right-side-up," the book invites the reader to join a trip to the city, journeying past ponds, farms, fields, trains, mountains, ocean waves, and bridges. Once in the city, the travelers enjoy its many entertainments and watch the sun set. By turning the book over, the reader takes the return trip home, marveling at birds that so recently were waves on the ocean and lightning flashes that were mountain roads when the book was "right-side-up." Jonas tests the perceptions of youngsters and shows them that things are not always what they might seem.

Relationship to Social Studies

The author's choice of subject matter makes *Round Trip* a natural addition to a third grade social studies program. Jonas investigates several examples of "community" in her work—urban, rural, small town, seaside, industrial, and agricultural. The book also suggests activities that build social studies-related skills in a number of key areas, including: map and globe, reflective thinking, communication, and time-order sequencing.

Jonas also implies a lesson that prospective citizens should learn—one should not always rely on first appearances when making a decision. Her visuals challenge students to investigate beyond the superficial, to determine the true nature of something before judging it. The book demands the curiosity and objectivity that an informed citizen demonstrates.

The book is readable for most third graders. The puzzling illustrations, moreover, guarantee students' involvement as they read the story individually or listen to it read aloud.

Developing Communication Skills

The notion of a "round trip" suggests activities in which students further their abilities to communicate ideas.

1. Read the story to students and discuss the notion of "round trips." Generate a list of "round trips" that people frequently take (i.e. visits to relatives, commuting to work, etc.); briefly discuss the reasons behind these travels. Divide children into groups of 3-4. Have group members take turns describing "round trips" that they have taken. To extend this activity, children may record their personal "round trip" in several short paragraphs. Have children adopt Jonas' spare style in writing these descriptions; post them on a bulletin board when finished.

2. After reading the story aloud and discussing its central idea, be sure that children understand a "round trip" and the reasons why people take them. Then, divide the class into work groups (about 3 children per group). Have each group write a short narrative describing the "round trip" that someone in your class takes to and from school. Then, have each group prepare a visual record of this "round trip" to accompany its story. Groups should use the most creative media available in your school (i.e. a videotape of the trip, a series of slides, a "home-made" filmstrip, etc.). Provide time for the groups to share and discuss their creations.

Nurturing the Affective Domain

Round Trip's affective dimension is not readily apparent. Jonas's story, for one thing, lacks characterizations or explicitly stated values for children to model. Yet, the work does suggest activities in which children make a judgment based on their own attitudes and then defend it. Read the book aloud, establish a chronology of events, then implement one of the following activities.

1. List the types of communities that the travelers encounter in Jonas's story. Guide children to the conclusion that these places can be grouped into two categories: "country places" and "city places." Ask children:
   a. Do the travelers like country or city places better?
   b. Do they like both areas equally well?
   c. How can you tell?
Conclude by asking children which they prefer and why.

2. As a follow-up to the first activity, have children state and defend their choice of country vs. city. Then, group like-minded children in work teams (3-4 per team). Have these small groups write a 30 second TV commercial supporting their choice in the country-city debate. Provide time for children to practice their scripts and gather simple props and costumes. Then, videotape each group's commercial. Share these videos in a large group session. If your school does not have VCR/camera equipment, have the groups present their commercials to the class as playlets.

Promoting
Thinking Skills

Round Trip introduces experiences that build students' abilities to classify, analyze, sequence, compare/contrast, and infer. Read the book to students and review the chronology of the story. Construct a timeline of major events. Then, implement one or more of the following activities.

1. Compile a list of the places and geographic features that the round-trippers encountered. Classify these items and label the categories that children create. Use these categories to draw inferences about the story's setting (i.e. an area with an unusual mix of features, rural blending into urban, etc.). Speculate with children where this round trip might have occurred based on an analysis of the categories.

2. As in the previous activity, list the places and geographic features shown in the story. Brainstorm a list of places and features that one would encounter on a day trip to and from your hometown. Compare/contrast these lists with students.

3. Reread the story, focusing on the travelers' reactions to the sights they experienced. Discuss these round trippers with the class. Then, divide students into small discussion groups (4-5 students each). Have these groups create profiles and pictures of Jonas's anonymous travelers. Share these descriptions with the entire class.

Using Map
and Globe Skills

The book suggests a number of activities that promote students' map and globe skills. Read the story aloud and discuss its main events. Review the places and geographic features that Jonas descibes. Then, consider the following lessons.

1. Divide students into trios and provide each threesome with a map of the U.S. Let the groups determine regions of the country in which the round trip might have occurred. Before the groups begin work, remind students of the geographic diversity the travelers encountered and the relatively short distance they journeyed (no more than 250 miles). Discuss the groups' conclusions as a class.

2. Divide students into small groups. Have each group construct an imaginary map of the area through which the round trippers traveled. Have the groups share their maps when completed.

3. Provide students with a day-long, round trip that they might take from your town. Divide them into pairs and provide each pair with a map of your area. Have the pairs: 1) trace the route they would take on this round trip on their maps; 2) determine places and geographic features they might see on this trip; 3) illustrate a view they might have from a car window during this journey. Allow students to share their pictures when finished.

Practicing
Social Interaction

After reading Jonas's book to the class, take the students on a "mini-round trip"—a walking tour out from and back to your school. For your round trip, choose as interesting a route as possible that can be walked in about half an hour. Remind students before they leave that they should be keen observers of the sights and sounds they encounter on their trip. Discuss the group walking tour after your return to the school. To extend this activity, consider the following lessons.

1. Small groups of students construct maps of their mini-round trip and display them around the classroom.

2. Small groups of students make books about their mini-round trip which may become part of the school library's collection.

3. A class photographer takes pictures along the walking tour. A bulletin board describing the walk may be constructed from these photos.

Appendix

CHILDREN'S FICTION AND THE SOCIAL STUDIES

A BIBLIOGRAPHY OF RESOURCES

A. Selecting Children's Books

These resources provide excellent guidance when selecting children's fiction appropriate for social studies teaching.

1. Carroll, Frances Laverne and Mary Meacham, eds. *Exciting, Funny, Scary, Short, Different, and Sad Books Kids Like About Animals, Science, Sports, Families, Songs and Other Things.* Chicago: ALA, 1984.

2. *Children's Books: Awards and Prizes.* New York: The Children's Book Council, 1986.

   This publication describes state "children's choice" awards. Potentially useful state awards listed in this publication include:

   Garden State Children's Book Award (New Jersey)

   Golden Archer Award (Wisconsin)

   Massachusetts Children's Book Award

   Pacific Northwest Library Association Young Reader's Choice, Award (AK, Alberta, WA, OR, MT, ID, and British Columbia)

   Mark Twain Award (Missouri)

   Young Hoosier Award (Indiana)

   Young Reader Medal (California)

3. "Children's Choices." International Reading Association.

   A preference list published every October in *The Reading Teacher*, the IRA's major journal. For single copies of the list, write to: IRA; ATTN: Children's Choices; P.O. Box 8139; Newark, Delaware 19714.

4. Schreiber, Joan. *Using Children's Books in Social Studies, Early Childhood Through Primary Grades.* Washington, D.C.: NCSS, 1984. (NCSS Bulletin 71).

5. "Notable Children's Trade Books in the Field of Social Studies." NCSS.

   Published in the April issue of *Social Education*. A tremendously useful resource prepared by the NCSS and the Children's Book Council.

6. Sorensen, Marilou R. (ed.) *Teaching Young People about the Law through Literature: An Annotated Bibliography.* ED 192 309.

B. Using Children's Fiction to Teach Social Studies

These resources provide practical tips for integrating children's fiction with a social studies program. They reflect a growing body of literature on this important teaching approach.

1. Bauer, Caroline Feller, *Handbook for Storytellers.* Chicago: ALA, 1977.

2. Billig, Edith, "Children's Literature as a Springboard to the Content Areas." *The Reading Teacher* (May 1977), 30 (8), 855-9.

3. Branson, Margaret Stimmann. *Tradebooks and the Social Studies: A Special Relationship.* Audiotape; part of the "Mini-Seminars on Using Books Creatively" Series. New York: Children's Book Council, 1979.

4. Brozo, William, and Carl Tomlinson. "Literature: The Key to Lively Content Courses." *The Reading Teacher* (Dec. 1986), 288-293.

5. Fassler, Joan, and Marjorie Graham Janis. "Books, Children, and Peace." *Children's Literature*, 2d Edition. Chicago: ALA, 1977.

6. Greene, Ellin, and Madalynne Schoenfeld, eds. *A Multimedia Approach to Children's Literature*, 2d Edition. Chicago: ALA, 1977.

7. Hennings, Dorothy G. "Reading Picture Storybooks in the Social Studies." *The Reading Teacher* (Dec. 1982), 36, 284-9.

8. Keach, Everett T., Jr. "Social Studies Instruction through Children's Literature." *Elementary School Journal* (Nov. 1974), 75 (2), 98-102.

HIEBERT LIBRARY

3 6877 00124 4747

9. *Learning Economics through Children's Stories,* 5th Edition. New York: Joint Council on Economic Education, 1986.

10. Levstik, Linda S. "Literary Geography and Mapping." *Social Education* (Jan. 1985), 49(1), 38-43.

11. McGowan, Tom, and Meredith McGowan. *Children, Literature, and Social Studies: Activities for the Intermediate Grades.* Indianapolis, IN: Special Literature Press, 1986.

12. Stoddard, Ann. *Teaching Social Studies in the Primary Grades with Children's Literature.* ED 251 848.

13. Trelease, Jim. *The Read-Aloud Handbook.* New York: Penguin Books, 1985.

14. Wheeler, Alan. "Individualizing Instruction in Social Studies through the Use of Children's Literature." *The Social Studies* (April 1971), 62 (4), 166-171.

C.   More Children's Books

KINDERGARTEN (Common Theme: "Understanding The Self")

Radlauer, Ruth Shaw. *Molly at the Library.* Illus. by Emily Arnold McCully. Simon & Schuster, 1988. 0-671-66166-3.

Rogers, Jean. *Runaway Mittens.* Pictures by Rie Munoz. Greenwillow, 1988. 0-688-07054-X.

Russo, Marisabina. *Only Six More Days.* Greenwillow, 1988. 0-688-07072-8.

Snyder, Zilpha Keatley. *Come On, Patsy.* Pictures by Margot Zemach. New York: Atheneum, 1982. 32 pp. ISBN 0-689-30892-2.

Stolz, Mary. *Storm in the Night.* Illus. by Pat Cummings. Harper, 1988. 0-06-025913-2.

Wilhelm, Hans. *Let's Be Friends Again!.* New York: Crown, 1986. 32 pp. ISBN 0-517-56252-9.

GRADE ONE (Common Theme: "Living Together in Families"):

Green, Phyllis. *Uncle Roland, the Perfect Guest.* Illustrated by Marybeth Farrell. New York: Four Winds Press, 1983. ISBN 0-590-07885-2.

Hest, Amy. *The Purple Coat.* Pictures by Amy Schwartz. New York: Four Winds Press, 1986. Unpaged (approximately 32 pp.). ISBN 0-02-743640-3.

Juke, Mavis. *Like Jake and Me.* Pictures by Lloyd Bloom. New York: Alfred A. Knopf, 1984. Unpaged (32 pp.). ISBN 0-394-95608-7.

Levinson, Riki. *Watch the Stars Come Out.* Illustrated by Diane Goode. New York: Dutton, 1985. Unpaged (28 pp.). ISBN 0-525-44205-7.

McPhail, David. *Sisters.* New York: Harcourt Brace Jovanovich, 1984. Unpaged (approximately 28 pp.). ISBN 0-15-275319-2.

GRADE TWO (Common Theme: "Discovering the Neighborhood"):

Hayes, Geoffrey. *Patrick and Ted.* New York: Four Winds press, 1984. Unpaged (32 pp.). ISBN 0-590-07902-6.

Hughes, Shirley. *Alfie Gives a Hand.* New York: Lothrop, Lee, and Shepard, 1983. ISBN 0-688-02387-8.

Weiss, Nicki. *Maude and Sally.* New York: Greenwillow Books, 1983. Unpaged (32 pp.). ISBN 0-688-01638-3.

GRADE THREE (Common Theme: "Learning Communities"):

Bang, Molly. *The Paper Crane.* New York: Greenwillow Books, 1985. Unpaged (approximately 30 pp.). ISBN 0-685-04109-4.

Daly, Niki. *Not So Fast, Songololo.* New York: Atheneum, 1986. Unpaged (25 pp.). ISBN 0-689-50367-9.

Godden, Rumer. *The Story of Holly and Ivy.* Pictures by Barbara Cooney. New York: Viking Kestrel, 1985. (32 pp.) ISBN 0-670-80622-6.